Career Focus Canada

CCP·SG·SDSM
-01

GEORGIAN | JOHN DI POCE
SOUTH GEORGIAN BAY
CAMPUS

499 Raglan Street, Collingwood, ON L9Y 3Z1
Phone 705.445.2961   Fax 705.445.1218

Career Focus Canada
A PERSONAL JOB SEARCH GUIDE

FIFTH EDITION

Helene Martucci Lamarre

Karen McClughan
LAMBTON COLLEGE

Pearson Canada
Toronto

Library and Archives Canada Cataloguing in Publication

Martucci Lamarre, Helene
        Career focus Canada : a personal job search guide / Helene Martucci Lamarre,
        Karen McClughan.—5th ed.

Includes index.
ISBN 978-0-13-609441-8

1. Job hunting—Canada.
I. McClughan, Karen, 1956– II. Title.

HF5382.75.C3M37 2010   650.14'0971   C2009-907092-8

Copyright © 2011, 2008, 2005, 2002, 1999 Pearson Canada Inc., Toronto, Ontario.

Pearson Prentice Hall. All rights reserved. This publication is protected by copyright and permission should be obtained from the publisher prior to any prohibited reproduction, storage in a retrieval system, or transmission in any form or by any means, electronic, mechanical, photocopying, recording, or likewise. For information regarding permission, write to the Permissions Department.

Original edition, entitled *Career Focus: A Personal Job Search Guide*, published by Pearson Education, Inc., Upper Saddle River, New Jersey, USA. Copyright © 2006 Pearson Education, Inc. This edition is authorized for sale only in Canada.

ISBN 978-0-13-609441-8

Vice-President, Editorial Director: Gary Bennett
Editor-in-Chief: Ky Pruesse
Editor, Humanities and Social Sciences: Joel Gladstone
Sponsoring Editor: Alexandra Dyer
Marketing Manager: Loula March
Assistant Editor: Jordanna Caplan
Production Editor: Melissa Hajek
Copy Editor: Jennifer McIntyre
Proofreaders: Melissa Hajek and Heather Sangster, Strong Finish Corp.
Production Coordinator: Sarah Lukaweski
Composition: MPS Limited, A Macmillan Company
Photo Researcher: Amanda Campbell
Art Director: Julia Hall
Cover Design: Quinn Banting
Cover Image: Martin Barraud/Getty Images

All photos from Hemera Technologies, © 2001, except photos on pages 11, 26, 87, 111 (by PhotoObjects), and on page 118 (by ShutterStock Images).

9 10 11 EBM 14 13 12

Printed and bound in the United States of America.

DEDICATION

This book is dedicated to all my wonderful canine companions who have brightened my life: Pepper, Muffin, Tara, Molly, and Abbey. They have demonstrated the meaning of loyalty and have taught me to take myself less seriously.

—Helene Martucci Lamarre

I would like to dedicate this text to the students that I have had the pleasure to work with. I hope I have contributed in a small way to your career success. May you all achieve your goals and dreams!

—Karen McClughan

CONTENTS

Welcome to the fifth edition of *Career Focus Canada: A Personal Job Search Guide*. In this book, you will be introduced to the world of personal assessment, personal marketing, and job-search know-how. By using this comprehensive yet easy-to-follow guide, you will gain a better understanding of who you are and the skills you offer employers. You will also learn how to launch your own personal marketing campaign and develop the all-important tools necessary for a successful job search in this competitive and complex world. You will learn what it takes to be successful after you get the job, identifying the skills and traits that are essential for success in any company or field of endeavour.

This personal marketing and job-search guide will help you focus more clearly on your abilities, your career aspirations, and your goals for the future. With its winning combination of career development theory and individual application, this book will assist you as you seek your first professional position, begin a new career, change careers, or even re-enter the job market after an absence. Whatever your career circumstances, through self-reflection and personal dedication, you can be on your way to career satisfaction. This exciting new edition retains most of the basic information that has been used so successfully by many job seekers, but it is enhanced with new and expanded information.

WHO SHOULD USE THIS BOOK?

Career Focus Canada: A Personal Job Search Guide, Fifth Edition, is a useful resource for everyone interested in employment. It is used as a textbook for college and professional career development courses. It is a valuable resource to individuals who are reassessing their careers and the effectiveness of their current job-search strategies. It has been a welcome companion to recent university, college, and technical school graduates who need career assistance as they make sense of the job market they are about to enter. Anyone who wishes to be successful in today's competitive employment market needs to understand and apply the ideas and techniques found in this guide.

HOW TO USE THIS BOOK

Use it actively. Don't just read the words—think about them. React to ideas, challenge your current ways of thinking, and energize yourself while you spend time with this book. As you think about how to use this guide most effectively for your individual situation, you may want to focus on particular sections, such as resumé writing, researching companies, or interviewing. Or, you may want to study the information and suggestions chapter by chapter as a comprehensive guide to personal marketing, successful job searching, and career planning. Learn about marketing tools, using the Internet in your job search, developing paper-based and electronic professional portfolios, and many other topics. No matter what your approach, you'll benefit from the experience, and this book will be a valuable tool for you today and in the future.

Approach

This fifth edition focuses on *self-marketing*. In fact, marketing yourself successfully is the focus of all the information found in the first two sections of the book. Experience tells us that today's job seekers are most successful when they understand basic marketing concepts and use dynamic marketing strategies and techniques for themselves.

Organization

- *MY Focus.* Because self-marketing is a central theme in this edition and is so central to a successful job search and career, marketing tips and other helpful information are highlighted in a special feature called "Marketing Yourself Focus," or MY Focus. MY Focus, found in Chapters 2–12, encourages the practical application of the ideas and suggestions in that chapter.
- *Finding Your Focus.* Chapters conclude with unique chapter questions, called Finding Your Focus. These questions encourage the reader to recall key concepts from the chapter and to reflect and apply these ideas on a personal level. Both MY Focus and Finding Your Focus help move the owner of this book from mere reader to active user of these critical concepts and job-search strategies.

Enhanced Information

The information in this book has been updated with the most timely career advice and strategies. New and expanded topics to this edition include:

- Types and styles of resumés, including targeted resumés
- Step-by-step instructions for converting your chronological resumé to a functional resumé
- Highlighted new resumé technology
- Enhanced behavioural-based interview information
- Career success on the job, including tips for new employees
- Expanded job safety information for new employees
- Comparison and discussion of generational differences
- Tips for working with difficult people
- Discussion of harassment in the workplace

Career Focus Canada: A Personal Job Search Guide remains an essential guide for anyone who is currently searching for a job or is about to begin a job search. Its no-nonsense approach and easy-to-read style make it a must for the busy individual who needs sound job search advice in a resource that is quick and easy to use.

Student Supplements

One very important feature of this fifth edition is the **Companion Website** (www.pearsoned.ca/lamarre). This interactive tool provides an online dimension of interactivity and self-exploration. The Companion Website features chapter objectives and highlights, test questions, useful Internet links, special worksheets, and further support information for the chapters in this book. Students can also use the Companion Website's Grade Tracker function to record and review their own progress on the self-graded quizzes.

CourseSmart for Students goes beyond traditional expectations–providing instant, online access to the textbooks and course materials you need at an average savings of 50 percent. With instant access from any computer and the ability to search your text, you'll find the content you need quickly, no matter where you are. And with online tools like highlighting and note-taking, you can save time and study efficiently. See all the benefits at www.coursesmart .com/students.

Instructor Supplements

The **Companion Website** (www.pearsoned.ca/lamarre) prepared for this textbook includes an exciting new function for instructors: Class Manager. This feature gives you the ability to quickly and easily monitor student progress on quizzes and other activities in an online gradebook. A variety of browse and search functions are available and allow you to quickly find any particular activity or student.

An **Instructor's Manual** contains lecture outlines and chapter outlines. All information has been thoroughly updated to reflect the new information in the text. The Instructor's Manual is available for downloading from a password-protected section of Pearson Education Canada's online catalogue (www. pearsoned.ca/highered). Navigate to your book's catalogue page to view a list of supplements that are available. See your local sales representative for details and access.

CourseSmart for Instructors goes beyond traditional expectations, providing instant, online access to the textbooks and course materials you need at a lower cost for students. And even as students save money, you can save time and hassle with a digital eTextbook that allows you to search for the most relevant content at the very moment you need it. Whether it's evaluating textbooks or creating lecture notes to help students with difficult concepts, CourseSmart can make life a little easier. See how when you visit www .coursesmart.com.

ACKNOWLEDGMENTS

I would like to thank the following reviewers, who offered helpful suggestions:

Lindsay Bett, Career Services Department, triOS College

Debbie Brannan, Faculty of Business, Seneca College

James Ellis, School of Agriculture and Environment, Assiniboine Community College

Dan Holbrook, School of Business, Centennial College

Karen Miller, Career Services Department, triOS College

Finally, I wish to thank the editors at Pearson Education Canada, for their encouragement and support of the fifth edition of *Career Focus Canada*.

—Karen McClughan

ABOUT THE AUTHORS

Helene Martucci Lamarre has successfully assisted job seekers for more than 20 years. As a senior professor, she has developed curricula and taught courses in career development and business communications to thousands of students who have attained an average placement rate of 97 percent. She is a distinguished professor, recognized for her creativity and academic contributions.

As a successful speaker, she has delivered numerous presentations to educational, civic, and private groups on career development and business communications topics. She also advises and coaches private clients in their personal job searches.

As an author, she has completed five books covering personal marketing, job-search techniques, and career portfolios published in both the United States and Canada.

She is a member of the Association for Business Communication and the Midwest Association of Colleges and Employers.

Karen McClughan has worked as a co-op and career consultant for over 21 years at the college level in Ontario, assisting both co-op students and graduates to successfully secure employment. During this time she has also developed curriculum and delivered job-search courses and workshops.

She has attained certification in Profiling Occupational Essential Skills.

She is a member of the following organizations:

- Ontario College Career Educators
- Education at Work Ontario
- Canadian Association of Career Educators and Employers
- Canadian Association for Co-operative Education

CHAPTER

1

Introduction: **Making Your Dreams Come True**

CHAPTER OBJECTIVES

After completing this chapter, you will be able to:

- Begin the journey toward career fulfillment.

- Learn about marketing yourself effectively.

- Review the steps of the job-search process.

All our dreams can come true—if we have the courage to pursue them.

—WALT DISNEY

You are about to take the first steps of one of the most important journeys you will ever take—the journey toward career fulfillment. Although you will travel many miles to make this dream come true, you know that the goal is worth the effort. This book will help you realize that dream. It will help you gain a clearer focus of yourself, your goals, your methods of achieving those goals, and your satisfaction with what you have achieved.

The various chapters teach you about self-assessment and promotion; the tools necessary to market yourself; techniques to consider before, during, and after an interview; tips on what to do after the job offer, including evaluating the offer; and suggestions for job success for the career changer as well as the new entry-level employee.

Because marketing yourself is so critical to your career success, this idea appears as a theme throughout the book with reminders of why and how self-marketing should be integrated into your career campaign. So, let's take a closer look at marketing yourself.

MARKETING YOURSELF

If you have ever taken a basic marketing course, you already know that to be a good seller of a product or service (or yourself!), you must understand the four Ps of marketing:

- product
- place
- promotion
- price

In an introductory marketing course, these concepts serve as a springboard for discussing and developing marketing strategies. If you developed a product and were preparing to sell it, you would have to consider the four Ps:

- What exactly is your product and how is it different from (or better than) other similar products?

- Where will you sell your product? Who are the potential buyers of the product and where are they?

1

- How will you let others know about your product and how will you develop its presentation to appropriate markets?
- How much should you charge for your product and how does that price compare to similar products being offered?

Product

These marketing basics are just as applicable to marketing yourself as they are to marketing a new product. For the purposes of this book, of course, that new product is you! Following is a discussion of these marketing concepts as they relate to your personal career development.

Let's start with a few simple questions, based on the four Ps: What are your features? What can you do well and how will hiring you be money wisely spent? What are some things you can't do? How will you get people interested in knowing what benefits there are to hiring you?

Place

Where do you intend to market yourself? Globally? Nationally? Regionally? Locally? Where will your buyers be? Is there anywhere you are unwilling to go? Must you keep your career search local? That's okay, but remember: the more broad-based your marketplace, the more opportunities you will have open to you. You should also be considering the environment or type of employer you want to work for. Do you want to work in an office environment, outdoors, for a small company or a large company? These are very important considerations to your job success.

Promotion

How will you introduce yourself to your markets, and how will you get people interested in considering you for employment? Although you likely won't take out a full-page advertisement in a national newspaper, you do have to find ways to let your buyers know that you have something to offer them. The first two promotional methods that come to mind are the cover letter and resumé. There is also your career portfolio, and the networking you do with various individuals who can help sell you to others.

Finally, the most important element of promotion is the interview. This is how you and your marketing tools will look and be judged—and here, perhaps most of all, presentation is absolutely essential. For example, how will your product be packaged (what will you wear to the interview)? How will you be groomed? How professional-looking will your resumé be? How about your cover letter and list of references? What kind of positive impression will your portfolio make during an interview? How about the manner and ease with which you answer various interview questions?

There is a lot of talk now about "branding." This simply means you need to determine what sets you apart, what your strengths are, and ensure that you are promoting these in your cover letters, resumés, and, of course, your interviews.

Price

This can be tricky. Of course, you want to earn the highest salary possible. At the same time, your buyers want value and do not want to overpay for the employees they hire. While most buyers will pay a competitive price for a good product, there are some employers who want to employ an individual for the lowest salary possible. So, how do you price yourself so you are able to close the sale? If you are a new graduate or entry-level employee, you don't have much of a yardstick to measure how much you are worth; however, you do want to be paid the same salary as someone else with your education and qualifications.

If you are making a career move or change, you want to be paid commensurate with your previous experience and responsibilities. A future salary range may be a bit easier to determine for the experienced employee based on current or previous salary. Regardless of your career level, however, you should have an idea of how much you need to earn, the average incomes for someone with your training and experience, and the average incomes found in your present or future geographical area. This information will help you determine what salary range you should use during the negotiating process.

FOUR P'S

You can see how important it is to use the four P's of marketing while planning a strategy to successfully market yourself. Planning and follow-through are critical to a successful marketing plan. Unfortunately, many job seekers merely post their resumés to online databases or send their resumés in response to newspaper ads and wait to see what happens. Most of the time, nothing does. The only result of this misguided approach is that the job seeker spends many an empty hour waiting for something to happen—not a good way to get the job you want.

Throughout this book, you will find self-marketing reminders and activities. They appear under the heading MY Focus. The "MY" means your own focus and a focus on *m*arketing *y*ourself. Assessing yourself and marketing yourself come into play in almost every aspect of your career campaign, from successful resumé writing to acing the interview.

JOB-SEARCH PROCESS

Now that you have looked at some marketing concepts and discovered how they relate to career success, let's put the job-search process in a visual perspective. Exhibit 1.1 depicts the steps of a successful career campaign that track with the

EXHIBIT 1.1	**The steps of a successful career campaign**

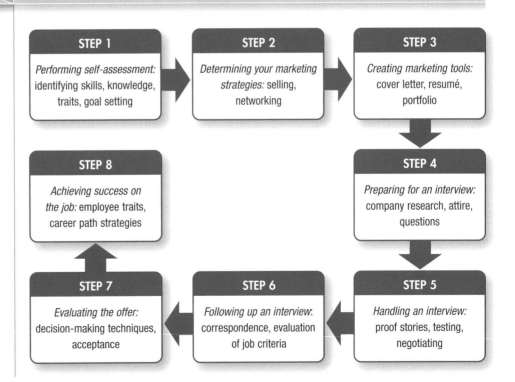

various sections and chapters of this book. Look over the chart. Think about the importance of these steps and how each one will take you closer to your destination: getting the job you want.

By completing this book, you will gain the knowledge, skills, and strengths necessary to ensure success at this and any stage of your career. The theories, advice, and tools are yours. The fun, the work, the achievements, the frustrations, and the triumph—it all starts here. With determination, perseverance, and a positive attitude about yourself and your talents, you *will* succeed.

2

Self-Assessment and Promotion: Knowing Yourself

CHAPTER OBJECTIVES

After completing this chapter, you will be able to:

- Determine your degree of readiness to sell yourself.

- Better understand who you are.

- Identify your abilities, skills, work values, and preferences.

- Apply your self-knowledge to your job search.

- Design a promotional strategy for your job search.

Only those who risk going too far can possibly find out how far one can go.

—T.S. ELIOT

SELF-ASSESSMENT

To be successful in any career search, it is imperative that you know yourself. Would a salesperson try to sell a product about which he or she knew little? Of course not. The same is true for a personal job search. First, take some time to think carefully about yourself. Unfortunately, many people are too busy, or perhaps too uncertain, to conduct a self-examination. This is a mistake. You must not skip this step of the process. If you do, your resumé will be weak, your research unfocused, and your interviewing skills substandard. That is not the way to conduct a successful job search. So, take some time to examine some important things about yourself and your life. You may be a young student with little experience, or a mature student making a career change, or a mature student without much of an employment history, but it is important to realize that all experience, whether life, employment, or volunteer, is relevant information to use when marketing yourself.

This chapter provides you with several self-assessment tools. A word of caution: these tools will not tell you everything you should know to make good career decisions. However, the insights gained from thinking about the issues raised in these self-assessment exercises can help you establish a strong, knowledgeable approach to your career development. You are encouraged to complete the following self-assessment tools:

- *Marketing Readiness Quiz:* Explore your views about selling yourself in the job market.

- *Self-Awareness Checklist:* See how you perceive yourself and others.

- *Ability Assessment:* Learn to recognize your talents and abilities.

- *Transferable Skills Checklist:* Compile a useful list of current skills that can transfer to new careers.

- *Work Environment and Preferences:* Identify lifestyle desires and work environment preferences that are important when choosing a job or career.

Once you have worked through each of them, complete the Self-Assessment Summary Sheet on page 19. In addition to these tools, several online self-assessment instruments are linked from the **Companion Website**.

MARKETING READINESS QUIZ

Do you have a "marketing or sales personality"? Are you "market-oriented" and "sales-minded"? According to career personnel, those are the qualities you must have to get the job of your choice. What follows is not a test of your sales knowledge; rather, it is a quiz to evaluate your sales personality and your attitude toward selling in general by asking you questions about selling yourself in the job market. Be honest with yourself as you take this quiz. Go with your instincts, not with what you think the answer should be. You can't fail this quiz; it is only meant as a guide to help you judge your sales readiness.

Directions

For each question, circle the response that best describes you. Then, use the Quiz Rating Scale at the end of the quiz to determine your score. Finally, use the Marketing Readiness Categories to determine how your score reflects your sales readiness.

1. You are planning a vacation with a friend. You want to go to Paris, and your friend wants to go on a cruise. Would you:
   A. Talk dynamically about Paris and what you love about it?
   B. Debate or ignore every reason he presents for going on the cruise?
   C. Try to find out what it is about the cruise that appeals to your friend the most?

2. What is the most difficult aspect of getting a job?
   A. Finding the right job opportunities
   B. Asking for the job at the interview
   C. Calling to make the appointment

3. When you picture a salesperson in your mind's eye, do you see:
   A. A person who is trying to help you solve a problem?
   B. An arm-twisting, aggressive salesperson?
   C. A smooth persuader whose main motive is to sell a product or service?

4. Your main goal at a job interview is:
   A. To get the job
   B. To get as much information as possible
   C. To ask questions

5. When you solve a major problem at work, do you:
   A. Go in and ask for a raise?
   B. Write it down and bring it up at performance appraisal time?
   C. Give it little notice and assume your boss is keeping an eye on all of your accomplishments?

6. You are planning to buy three pairs of expensive shoes in a small store, or three pieces of expensive electronic equipment. Do you:

   A. Pay for them without any discussion?

   B. Ask at the outset whether you will get a discount if you buy all three?

   C. Say, after trying on shoes or examining the equipment for some time, "I might buy all three if you give a discount"?

7. The last time someone said no to you, did you:

   A. Ask why she said no?

   B. Take the no as an irrevocable decision?

   C. Keep trying to persuade her to say yes?

8. When you are in a group of very aggressive, talkative people, do you:

   A. Hold your own comfortably?

   B. Sit back timidly, content to listen?

   C. Speak up occasionally because you don't want to be left out?

9. If someone asks you to describe your best feature, do you:

   A. Talk non-stop for hours?

   B. Blush and not know where to start?

   C. Briefly discuss two or three admirable traits?

10. If you hear about a job opening, do you:

    A. Send a resumé?

    B. Call personnel to get more information?

    C. Try to contact the person you'd actually be working for?

11. How do you prepare for a job interview?

    A. Role-play with friends or colleagues

    B. Develop a list of questions to ask

    C. Think about what you'll be asked and prepare some answers

12. When sending out a letter with your resumé to a prospective employer, do you:

    A. Send a form letter?

    B. Think about not sending a letter?

    C. Write a tailored letter for each job?

13. If you call a prospective employer and he immediately says, "We're not hiring today," what do you think is the reason for that statement?

    A. The employer took an instant dislike to you

    B. It's not the right time

    C. He doesn't have a good reason to talk to you

14. If you are selling computers and need customers, do you:

    A. Call up all of your friends?

    B. Attend a seminar on "Computer Basics for Small Business Owners"?

    C. Open a phone book and start cold calling?

15. You applied for a job you really wanted and were turned down by Human Resources personnel. Do you:

    A. Call and try to get another appointment?

    B. Accept the decision and try another company?

    C. Try to find out to whom you would report and make an appointment directly with that person?

16. Why do you think people "buy"?

    A. Because it makes them feel good

    B. Because their buying is based on a logical decision

    C. Because they like the salesperson

17. You are going on an important interview. Do you:

    A. Research the company?

    B. Wing it?

    C. Decide that you'll ask questions during the interview to learn what you need to know?

18. A friend gives you a referral. Do you:

    A. Take the name and number and say, "I'll call next week"?

    B. Take the name and number and call immediately?

    C. Ask your friend for more information about the job and the boss?

19. Why is listening such an important part of the sales process?

    A. To get important information

    B. To find out the hidden concerns

    C. To show that you care

20. What is the best way to stay in control during a sales presentation or a job interview?

    A. Always have planned questions

    B. Keep talking in a very persuasive manner

    C. Answer every objection or concern raised

21. At the end of a job interview, do you:

    A. Say thank you and leave?

    B. Ask for the job?

    C. Ask when you'll be hearing from the employer?

22. You've been searching for a job for six months and have been rejected 20 times. Do you:

    A. Get angry and take it out on friends and family?

    B. Begin to doubt your own abilities?

    C. Re-evaluate your interviewing skills?

23. In an interview situation, which do you view as a strong signal of acceptance?

    A. The interviewer asks, "When can you start?"

    B. The interviewer says, "This would be your desk."

    C. The interview goes on for a long time.

24. You receive a memo from a colleague complimenting your performance. Do you:

    A. Show it to your family, friends, and colleagues?

    B. Acknowledge it, feel good, and stash it away?

    C. Make copies and send it to your boss, her boss, and even the company president?

25. Who do you think gets to the top in most organizations?

    A. People who work the hardest

    B. People who fit into the corporate culture

    C. People who sell themselves most effectively

For each response, assign the point value indicated. Read the related discussion for each, then add up your total points.

1.   A = 3   B = 1   C = 5

The worst way to sell anything is to ignore or argue with the other person (B). This only hurts his feelings or makes him want to cling stubbornly to his position. Talking dynamically about Paris (A) may help, but the real secret to selling is to appeal to what the other person wants or needs. By finding out what's most appealing about the cruise (C), you'll learn what the other person really wants. If he says, "There's a lot of dancing on board ship," for instance, you can counter with a list of places to go dancing in Paris.

2.   A = 3   B = 5   C = 3

Even the most experienced salespeople sometimes have difficulty "asking for the order" (B). When you're in an interview (the ultimate sales situation), an essential sales skill is knowing how to be assertive without being aggressive. Finding job opportunities (A) is not difficult if you take advantage of research tools available in the papers and the library, and personal contacts. Calling to make the appointment (C), also an important skill, is not difficult if you use three Ps: patience, practice, and perseverance.

3.   A = 5   B = 0   C = 1

Your own notion of what a salesperson is determines your ability to succeed in today's job market. If you see salespeople as arm twisters (B), you won't feel very good about having to sell yourself. If you see a person who's trying to help you solve a problem (A), that's the kind of salesperson you'll be during your job hunt. Smooth persuaders (C) usually do well in this world, but they typically finish second to someone genuinely concerned with solving other people's problems.

4.   A = 5   B = 5   C = 5

All three of these answers are good, but one is better than the others. You want to come away with a job offer so you can decide whether or not to take the job (A). You want to get as much information as possible so you can make a smart decision about the job (B). The best answer is to go in prepared to ask questions (C) in order to accomplish A and B.

5.   A = 5   B = 3   C = 1

If you go right in and ask for a raise, you're sales oriented and interested in building your value (A). This is the best approach, in step with today's more assertive approach to life. Waiting for performance appraisal time is good (B), but that may be a long time off. One philosophy is that it's more important to keep yourself in the eye of the organization. You do this by letting people know when you've done something valuable. If you give it little notice (C), no one else will notice it either. If you don't sell yourself, nobody else will.

6.   A = 1   B = 3   C = 5

Negotiation is an important selling skill. The best time to ask for a discount is after a salesperson has invested time showing her wares (C). At that point, she'd rather give you a deal than lose the sale. You get three points for asking for a discount when you come in (B). You're on the right track, but you don't want to tip your hand at the beginning. You get one point for being successful enough to afford paying full price for the three items (A).

7.   A = 5   B = 1   C = 3

It's important to know why someone says no (A) if you want to get a yes the next time. It might even tell you how to change the no to a yes this time. If you keep trying to make the sale (C), you're not easily dissuaded and have enough confidence in yourself to try again. If you take every no as an irrevocable decision (B), you're not giving yourself a chance to learn what your mistake might have been.

8.   A = 5   B = 2   C = 3

Congratulations on holding your own (A) and feeling comfortable about it. Competition for jobs will be great, and the better your communications skills, the easier you'll find it is to sell yourself and increase your chances of getting the jobs you want. Speaking up occasionally (C) gets you three points for realizing that you should make an effort to participate. You get two points for listening

(B) because you may gain valuable information. But you have to learn to hold your own in a conversation if you're going to compete in the job market.

9.   A = 1   B = 3   C = 5

Talking non-stop about your product (in this case, you) is not a very effective sales technique (A). Your customers will see you as pushy or unconcerned with their welfare. If you blush and don't know where to start (B), it means you're unprepared for the question. You wouldn't start selling cars without knowing anything about them, so prepare yourself for the questions your customers will most likely ask. If your answer was (C), it shows you think enough of yourself to discuss your good qualities without being obnoxious.

10.   A = 1   B = 2   C = 5

If you emulate successful salespeople, you'll take the initiative, be more assertive, and go directly to the person who makes the final hiring decision (C). Because you've heard about the position, use your source to get your foot in the door: "Johnny Jones suggested I call." Calling Human Resources to get more information (B) is less helpful but shows you're willing to do some research. If you just send a resumé to Human Resources (A), you're not taking advantage of your inside knowledge.

11.   A = 5   B = 5   C = 5

This is a question where all three answers are good. Doing well at job interviews takes skill, and the way to build a skill is to be prepared and practise, practise, practise.

12.   A = 2   B = 0   C = 5

Sending a resumé with no cover letter at all (B) tells a potential employer that you have no special interest in him or his company. The sales-oriented approach is to let the employer know why he should read the resumé and call you in for an interview. You do this by sending a letter tailored specifically for him (C). Sending a form letter is almost as bad as no letter at all (A).

13.   A = 1   B = 3   C = 5

In selling terms, you've encountered sales resistance in this situation, which occasionally occurs when the customer doesn't like the salesperson (A). But in this case, you haven't spoken long enough for the employer to dislike you (unless you were rude or obnoxious). It's possible that the employer was busy and you caught him at a bad time (B). But the most common reason for resistance is that the salesperson hasn't established the value of the product or service (C)— in other words, hasn't presented a strong enough reason for the customer to buy (or for the employer to keep talking to you). If this happens often when you call, it means you should change your approach.

14.   A = 4   B = 5   C = 1

Calling all of your friends (A) is an excellent way to start because networking is one of the best ways to find buyers for your product. Attending a seminar for new business owners (B) shows you have strong sales sensibilities. People who

attend such seminars are "qualified" buyers; they're definitely in the market for your product, so your chances of making a sale here are very good. Just opening the phone book (C) and making calls may bring you a few customers, but you'll probably waste most of your time and effort. In the job search, the more qualified buyers you reach, the better your chances of getting the job you want.

15. A = 3 B = 0 C = 5

If you have been turned down by personnel and just accept this decision (B), you are too easily discouraged. Successful salespeople try to close the sale (get the person to buy) at least five times before they even consider giving up. Going directly to the decision maker (C) demonstrates sales smarts and persistence, both necessary and desirable qualities for the job-search process. Trying to get another appointment through personnel (A) is not as effective, but does show you're resilient and not easily put off.

16. A = 5 B = 1 C = 3

Emotions play a big part in both the selling and hiring processes. People buy (or hire) for emotional reasons (A); the product fulfills a need or desire they have. That's why, in order to sell yourself to an employer, you'll have to show him how you'll solve his problems or fulfill his needs. People also buy from people they like, trust, and respect (C). You can't make someone like you, but you can show that you are a person worthy of trust and respect. Logic almost always plays a lesser role in the decision-making process (B).

17. A = 5 B = 0 C = 3

Although asking questions (C) is an essential part of the interview process, most people are impressed by what you already know about them. Before you go on a "sales call," learn as much as you can about the company and the person you're going to see (A). You'll stand out from other applicants. If you try to wing it (B), you put yourself at a definite disadvantage—you'll know nothing about the company or the job before sitting down with the interviewer.

18. A = 1 B = 3 C = 5

The best answer in this case is to ask your friend for more information before you make the call (C). You want to find out something about the person you'll be calling (who she is, what her position is in the company, etc.), what the job is like, and why this job is open. Calling immediately (B) shows you have initiative, but you'd be better off researching the company first. If you say, "I'll call next week" (A), you're probably just putting it off and may lose the opportunity.

19. A = 5 B = 5 C = 5

All three answers are good. There's an old saying that "Customers don't care how much you know until they know how much you care." In a hiring situation, the interviewer wants to know how much you care about the job and the company (C). Listening carefully also gives you important factual information (A) and may reveal the hidden concerns of the individual interviewer (B), the real reasons you will or won't get hired.

20.   A = 5   B = 1   C = 3

Here is an important sales maxim: "The person who asks the questions controls the conversation." Going into the interview with a series of planned questions (A) keeps you in control of the situation and makes sure you get all of the information you need to make a smart decision. What you think is talking in a persuasive manner (B) may come across as conceited and pushy. Without asking questions, you could end up talking for hours and never satisfy the employer's real concerns. Clearly, answering objections or concerns (C) is essential to a successful interview, but that doesn't give you the same control that asking questions does.

21.   A = 1   B = 5   C = 3

It's important that you "ask for the sale" or, in this case, the job (B). Ask in a pleasant, civil way so that you don't turn people off. Saying thank you and leaving (A) is not going to help you get the job unless you're the most sought-after person in the world. Asking when you'll be hearing from the employer (C) shows a little more assertiveness and is better than just saying thanks and leaving. But more than likely you'll be told, "We have several candidates to choose from. We'll call you."

22.   A = 0   B = 1   C = 5

The best answer here is to re-evaluate your interviewing skills (C). Twenty interviews can give you a lot of good experience in different situations that may arise. Go over your experiences and ask yourself what you did right and what can be improved. If you begin to doubt your own abilities (B), you're taking rejection too personally. A negative decision may have nothing to do with your personality. Getting angry at yourself or at anyone else (A) doesn't improve your skills or your chances at the next interview. Don't give up trying; the next interview could be the one you've been waiting for!

23.   A = 3   B = 5   C = 1

Most people take a long interview as a sign of definite interest (C). In fact, this often signifies nothing more than a disorganized interviewer, someone who doesn't really know what he's looking for. Don't assume an hour-long interview means you're going to be hired. If, however, the interviewer starts to visualize you in the job and refers to "your" desk or "your" co-workers (B), that is a pretty good clue that there is a strong interest. "When can you start?" (A) is a possible sign of interest, but it may also indicate that the employer is in urgent need of someone and may not be able to wait until you're available.

24.   A = 3   B = 1   C = 5

Are you secure enough to take hold of your future and make sure the right people see what others think of you? Because only the rich and famous have public relations agents, you have to assume that role for yourself. The best answer is (C). Showing the letter to your friends and colleagues (A) will make you feel better and perhaps add to your reputation but may not do much where your boss is concerned. Feeling good is always nice (B), but why pass up opportunities to increase your visibility?

25.   A = 3   B = 4   C = 5

Although we're in the middle of the information age, we're also at the beginning of the age of marketing. Even political candidates have to "sell" themselves if they want to get elected. You must be well versed in sales and marketing skills to get ahead (C). Corporate fit is and will continue to be important (B), but work is becoming less structured in many situations. Hard workers (A) are not to be discounted, but they are not necessarily the people who get ahead. In a small or newly organized company, this may be the case, but unless other people know how hard you work, or unless you "fit in" with the rest of the team, your hard work will not always be appreciated.

Marketing Readiness Categories

96–125 points

Good for you! You've scored high in sales readiness, which means you're one step ahead of the competition already. You have a positive attitude toward selling and a personality that makes you a natural for marketing yourself!

71–95 points

You are well on your way toward the sales and marketing orientation required for success in today's market. You're thinking in the right direction, and with just a little improvement, there'll be no stopping you!

46–70 points

You're not quite at the level you should be, but you're getting there. You should be a bit more assertive and have more confidence in yourself. All it takes is a shift in attitude and a willingness to learn. You're on the right track.

45 points or less

You need to re-evaluate your attitudes and perceptions regarding sales and marketing. Doing the exercises and following the advice in this book will help improve your readiness to market yourself and increase your job-search know-how.

How well did you score as a salesperson or marketing expert? What did you learn about yourself? Are there any aspects of selling yourself that need improvement? Write your thoughts below, focusing on ways to strengthen your sales and marketing readiness.

_____

_____

_____

_____

_____

_____

_____

_____

_____

SELF-AWARENESS CHECKLIST

An important part of self-assessment is self-awareness. How aware are you of the ways you perceive yourself and others? How much do you know about the ways you react to situations? To determine your level of self-awareness, read the statements below and place an X in the circle that corresponds to how often you feel this way. Use this page to help you think about how you perceive yourself and how you wish to be perceived.

	Always	Often	Sometimes	Rarely	Never
I am eager to learn.	○	○	○	○	○
My work is exciting.	○	○	○	○	○
I'm willing to listen with an open mind.	○	○	○	○	○
I constantly have new insights.	○	○	○	○	○
I like taking direction from people who know something I don't.	○	○	○	○	○
I try to look at the world through the eyes of the other person.	○	○	○	○	○
When someone is talking to me, I really listen.	○	○	○	○	○
I'm honest with myself and others.	○	○	○	○	○
I've thought about my own strengths and weaknesses.	○	○	○	○	○
I'm sensitive to others' needs.	○	○	○	○	○
I care for and am concerned about others.	○	○	○	○	○
I adapt easily to the environment and situation.	○	○	○	○	○
I am willing to take risks.	○	○	○	○	○
I am satisfied with the way I look physically.	○	○	○	○	○
I am satisfied with the way I feel physically.	○	○	○	○	○

ABILITY ASSESSMENT

In our day-to-day lives, we often don't take time to make a serious assessment of ourselves. This is critical to conducting a successful job search. In the following exercise, you will look at what you consider to be your talents and examine a variety of ability areas in an attempt to pinpoint your unique qualities.

The ability categories are defined on the following pages. Evaluate yourself on each of these according to the following scale:

   1 = No ability at all
   2 = Enough ability to get by with some help
   3 = Some natural ability
   4 = Definite, strong ability
   5 = Outstanding ability

Try not to compare yourself with any particular reference group such as other students, other colleagues, or the general population. Just rate yourself according to your best assessment of your individual capability.

VERBAL/PERSUASIVE

_____ *Writing:* express self well in writing

_____ *Talking:* express self well in ordinary conversation

_____ *Speaking:* deliver a speech, address an audience

_____ *Persuading:* convince others of your view

_____ *Selling:* convince others to purchase a product or service

_____ *Negotiating:* bargain or assist in the bargaining process

SOCIAL

_____ *Social ease:* relax and enjoy social situations such as parties or receptions

_____ *Appearance:* dress appropriately and presentably for a variety of interpersonal or group occasions

_____ *Self-esteem:* maintain a positive view of self, including accepting negative feedback or criticism

_____ *Dealing with public:* continually relate to a broad cross section of people who need information, service, or help

TECHNICAL

_____ *Computational speed:* manipulate numerical data rapidly and accurately without using any mechanical device

_____ *Working with data:* comfortably work with large amounts of data; compile, interpret, and present such data

_____ *Computer use:* use computers to solve problems, knowledge of programming, and familiarity with various computer capabilities

INVESTIGATIVE

_____ *Scientific curiosity:* comfortable with scientific method of inquiry, knowledge of scientific phenomena

_____ *Research:* gather information in a systematic way for a certain field of knowledge

CREATIVE

_____ *Artistic:* sensitivity to aesthetics, create works of art

_____ *Use imagination:* create new ideas or forms with various physical objects

_____ *Use imagination:* create new ideas by merging abstract ideas in new ways

WORKING WITH OTHERS

_____ *Supervisory:* oversee, direct, and manage work of others

_____ *Teaching:* help others learn how to do something or to understand something, provide insight

_____ *Coaching:* instruct or train for improvement of performance

_____ *Counselling:* develop helping relationship with another individual

MANAGERIAL

_____ *Organization and planning:* develop a program, project, or set of ideas with systematic preparation and arrangement of tasks; coordinate people and resources as well

_____ *Orderliness:* arrange items in a regular fashion so that information is readily retrieved and used

_____ *Handling details:* work with a variety or volume of information without losing track

_____ *Making decisions:* comfortably make judgments or reach conclusions about matters that require action; accept responsibility for the consequences of such actions

Now that you have reflected on your abilities, decide which ones you believe represent your most prominent strengths. Refer to those areas that have 4s and 5s. Now, choose which are your most outstanding and noteworthy abilities and list them below. Remember these as you continue to focus on the personal abilities and skills you have to offer an employer.

_____

_____

_____

TRANSFERABLE SKILLS CHECKLIST

Transferable skills are those general competencies that you have developed from previous jobs, volunteer work, or life experiences. These competencies are very valuable when marketing yourself to employers—especially if you are a recent college graduate with little direct business or industry experience. These skills, gained in other settings, will be transferred into the new position you seek. Review the list of transferable skills that follows and check the ones you feel you have. Keep these transferable skills in mind because you will use a similar checklist when resumé preparation is discussed later. Use the two checklists to help you write a resumé that will promote your worth to a potential employer.

___ Advise people   ___ Check for accuracy

___ Analyze data   ___ Coach

___ Anticipate problems   ___ Collect money

___ Arrange functions   ___ Communicate (in writing)

___ Assemble things   ___ Communicate (verbally)

___ Audit records   ___ Construct

___ Budget money   ___ Consult with others

___ Buy products or services   ___ Coordinate activities

___ Calculate and manipulate   ___ Cope with deadlines
    numbers

(Continued)

___ Correspond	___ Learn quickly
___ Create	___ Listen
___ Delegate	___ Make decisions
___ Demonstrate	___ Make policy
___ Demonstrate responsibility	___ Manage a business
___ Design	___ Manage people
___ Develop	___ Mediate problems
___ Direct others	___ Meet deadlines
___ Do precise work	___ Meet goals
___ Drive a vehicle	___ Meet the public
___ Edit	___ Memorize information
___ Encourage	___ Mentor others
___ Endure long hours	___ Negotiate
___ Enforce	___ Nurture
___ Evaluate	___ Observe
___ Examine	___ Organize
___ File records	___ Pay attention to detail
___ Find information	___ Perceive needs
___ Follow directions	___ Perform customer service
___ Follow through	___ Perform public relations duties
___ Handle complaints	___ Persuade others
___ Handle equipment	___ Plan
___ Handle money	___ Program
___ Help people	___ Protect property
___ Implement	___ Raise money
___ Improve	___ Research
___ Install	___ Sell
___ Interpret data	___ Set goals
___ Interview people	___ Solve problems
___ Investigate	___ Write reports
___ Lead people	

WORK ENVIRONMENT AND LIFE PREFERENCES

When making a career decision, it is important to look at work environment and life preferences. If you identify areas that are important to you, this can guide you to a position with which you will be satisfied.

The following inventory lists work environment and life preferences. Reflect on what is really important to you in these areas and indicate your preferences.

Place an X in the circle that reflects the degree of importance for that item. If you strongly prefer to be self-employed, for question #1, put your X over the 2 on the left. If you are neutral about whether you work alone or with people, place your mark for question #2 over the zero. If you have a strong preference for a structured environment, place your mark for question #3 over the 2 on the right.

	2	1	0	1	2	
1. Self-employed	②	①	⓪	①	②	Work in a company
2. Work with others	②	①	⓪	①	②	Work alone
3. Creative environment	②	①	⓪	①	②	Structured environment
4. No supervision	②	①	⓪	①	②	Close supervision
5. Extended work hours	②	①	⓪	①	②	Standard eight-hour day
6. Similar duties daily	②	①	⓪	①	②	Variety of duties
7. Structured work	②	①	⓪	①	②	Creative work
8. Flexible hours	②	①	⓪	①	②	Regular hours
9. Overtime desired	②	①	⓪	①	②	No overtime work
10. Security	②	①	⓪	①	②	Challenge, risk
11. Slow pace, little pressure	②	①	⓪	①	②	Fast pace, high pressure
12. Little, no travel	②	①	⓪	①	②	Frequent travel
13. Opportunity for relocation	②	①	⓪	①	②	No relocation
14. Small business	②	①	⓪	①	②	Large business
15. Live in rural area	②	①	⓪	①	②	Live in urban area
16. Desire culture/ community	②	①	⓪	①	②	Little need for culture/community
17. Spend money	②	①	⓪	①	②	Save money
18. Material things matter	②	①	⓪	①	②	Material things don't matter
19. Live close to family members	②	①	⓪	①	②	Live anywhere
20. Marry/children	②	①	⓪	①	②	Single life

SELF-ASSESSMENT SUMMARY SHEET

Now, let's take a look at how you did with your self-assessment work.

1. What was your score on the Marketing Readiness Quiz? Based on this sales ability score, will you have to make adjustments in the way you approach marketing yourself for a job?

_____

_____

2. Now that you have completed the Ability Assessment, in what ability area(s) are you strongest? How can you use this knowledge to market yourself in your chosen career? What ability area(s) are your weakest? How can you work at improving these?

_____

_____

_____

3. Using the results of the Transferable Skills Checklist, what are the top three transferable skills you possess? How might you showcase these on your resumé or during an interview?

_____

_____

_____

4. What work environment and life preferences are most important to you? In what ways might these preferences affect your career decision making?

_____

_____

_____

SELF-PROMOTION

All of the self-assessment in the world won't help you achieve your career goals unless you know how to promote yourself. The tighter the job market, the greater the need to market! Later chapters will help you prepare the marketing tools necessary for a successful marketing campaign, but for now let's take a look at some other aspects of selling yourself.

When you were young, you may have been taught by your parents not to boast or brag about yourself because it wasn't appropriate or polite. So, somewhere deep in your psyche, you may feel that you shouldn't toot your own horn. Or maybe you think that your actions speak for you. This may be true for people who know you and like you and your work, but what about those who don't know you? What about those whom you are trying to convince to give you a job? How are these individuals going to learn what you are capable of doing unless you tell them?

Self-promotion is essential if you wish to secure the job you want, and if you wish to advance in that job in the future. You must get past any thoughts you have about not talking or bragging about yourself. Indeed, that's basically what a job search is all about: bragging about yourself! But it is bragging with facts to back up what you say. As indicated earlier, throughout this book the MY Focus feature (MY Focus = marketing yourself focus) will highlight ways to market yourself. To implement MY Focus, read the advice in the box on page 22.

Just what is it that employers are looking for? Of course, they want you to be qualified for the positions they have open. Your basic qualifications are probably your diploma or degree, additional training, and work experience. But what other skills or traits do employers seek? The list of skills in the box on page 23 was developed by Randall S. Hansen and Katharine Hansen for their article "What Do Employers Really Want? Top Skills and Values Employers Seek from Job-Seekers." The entire article can be found on their website, Quintessential Careers, at www.quintcareers.com/job_skills_values.html.

Finally, you should start thinking of where you can promote yourself and who can help you. This is discussed in detail in the chapter on selling techniques. For now, however, think about the people who can help you in your job search. Certainly, immediate family, friends, and current or previous employers can assist. But also think about the not-so-obvious people you may encounter on a daily basis, especially those who also see many people because of the type of work they do.

For example, what about your doctor or dentist? How about the person who cuts your hair or your dry cleaner? What about the people who work at one of your favourite restaurants or the person who fixes your car? These are people who might know someone in your field or someone who knows someone else. The more people you tell that you are engaged in a job search, the more your network can grow. And the more your network grows, the closer you are to getting the job you want.

Understanding Essential Skills

Essential Skills are the skills needed for work, learning, and life. They provide the foundation for learning all other skills and enable people to evolve with their jobs and adapt to workplace change.

Through extensive research, the Government of Canada and other national and international agencies have identified and validated nine Essential Skills. These skills are used in nearly every occupation and throughout daily life in different ways and at different levels of complexity.

There are nine Essential Skills:

- Reading Text
- Document Use
- Numeracy
- Writing
- Oral Communication
- Working with Others
- Continuous Learning
- Thinking Skills
- Computer Use

Copyright by Human Resources and Social Development Canada. "Human Resources and Skills Development Canada—Essential Skills" can be found at http://srv108.services.gc.ca/english/general/Understanding_ES_e.shtml. Reproduced with the permission of Her Majesty the Queen in Right of Canada 2006.

These Essential Skills are important for you to be aware of and will be useful in a number of areas. You should use the website below to search for your career choice or positions you have held in the past. The descriptions and ratings will be useful in creating your marketing documents for your job search. Once you become familiar with Essential Skills you will also notice that many employers and job posting sites will use Essential Skills in job postings.

In addition, you will also find that some employers will test for competency in pre-employment testing or when determining promotions within a company. You will be hearing much more about Essential Skills in the future as the practice becomes more common.

INTERNET SOURCES

Human Resources and Social Development Canada Essential Skills website: http://srv108.services.gc.ca/english/general/Understanding_ES_e.shtml

MY Focus — ESPECIALLY FOR COLLEGE STUDENTS

- It is critically important to get to know yourself. Be self-aware, assess your abilities, identify personality traits and personal skills, and figure out what you value in work and life.

- Understand that no one else can get the job for you. You must market yourself successfully. In order to do that, you must brag about yourself and support your bragging with facts and experiences.

- Realize that most job openings (and this is especially true in a tighter job market) are discovered through personal networking and marketing.

- Discover what employers are looking for when they commit to hiring new employees. Then, develop an effective way to convince the hiring authority that you have the qualities they seek and that you are the best person for the job!

Skills Most Sought After by Employers

- *Ability to communicate:* Listening, speaking, and writing

- *Ability to analyze/research:* Assessing a situation, gathering information, drawing conclusions

- *Ability to use technology:* Computer literacy, technical competence

- *Ability to be flexible and adaptable, and able to multitask:* Adjusting to change, managing multiple tasks, setting priorities

- *Ability to build good interpersonal relations:* Relating to and inspiring others, handling conflict

- *Ability to lead or manage:* Taking charge when necessary and supervising people and/or tasks

- *Ability to be sensitive to multicultural issues:* Handling diversity and being aware of and sensitive to others from different cultures

- *Ability to plan and organize:* Designing, planning, and implementing projects and tasks

- *Ability to work in a team:* Using a professional approach when working with others and building trusting relationships with co-workers and others

Copyright by Quintessential Careers. The original article, "What Do Employers Really Want?", can be found at www.quintcareers.com/job_skills_values.html. Reprinted with permission.

FINDING YOUR FOCUS

1. Why is it important to do a self-assessment before beginning a job search?

2. How does a self-assessment improve the job-search process? What tools benefit from good self-reflection?

3. Based on the Self-Assessment Summary Sheet, what are two or three of your strongest skills or traits that you can use to market yourself?

4. Are you open to aggressive self-promotion? If so, how will you develop your network? If not, what issues must you overcome in order to be open to self-promotion?

CHAPTER

Marketing Strategies

CHAPTER OBJECTIVES

After completing this chapter, you will be able to:

- Develop a personal marketing plan.

- Use informational interviewing to secure information and develop relationships.

- Use electronic resources as an effective means of self-marketing.

- Apply a proactive approach and positive attitude to your career development.

- Develop and use a systematic strategy for marketing yourself to companies.

Focusing on Your Market

Keep your face to the sunshine and you cannot see the shadows.

—HELEN KELLER

A marketing plan or selling strategy has many components. The aspects of selling yourself covered here include personal marketing, interviewing for information, tapping into electronic resources, determining the best approach, developing a positive attitude, and examining a systematic strategy to pursue various companies or hiring authorities.

TAKE ADVANTAGE OF PERSONAL MARKETING

Earlier chapters discussed the need for marketing yourself, but how is this really accomplished? How will you let others know about you, your skills, and your talents? Every day thousands of job seekers circle classified advertisements in newspapers and find potential positions in online databases. And every day the same thousand people send off cover letters and resumes, hoping to receive replies. Usually, they don't. There is nothing personal about this approach, and, for the most part, it just doesn't work.

Nothing beats personal contact. There are two obvious benefits of personally contacting people and developing leads: you become aware of openings that are not placed in newspapers and online, and you become a specific person with an identity, not just a face in the crowd. Case in point—consider the hidden job market. Ever heard of it?

The hidden job market is the market that few people really know or think about. It is the opposite of the published job market. The published job market is the one that those thousands of people mentioned earlier are trying to use. You know the one: the job market that is advertised through classified ads and postings, online databases, recruiter listings, and marketing websites. Job-search experts say that only about 20 percent of available jobs are advertised through these means. Another problem with this marketplace is that most people use it and, oftentimes, the best jobs are not marketed through these channels at all.

24

In contrast, the hidden job market is very real and vibrant. This is the marketplace where up to 80 percent of the openings exist. This is the marketplace that you can tap by making yourself known to many people through networking and other means. You can do this face to face, by using the telephone or e-mail, and by attending professional organization events in your field. You see, this market is exclusive to those who come recommended or referred by others, often others who are already in the company or field. These individuals are given preferential treatment as candidates. They are already "prescreened," so to speak. So, where would you rather spend your time? Trying to get a job in the advertised job market or in the hidden job market?

Where Do You Want to Be?

- *Advertised job market:* Used by 80 percent of candidates; includes 20 percent of the jobs
- *Hidden job market:* Used by 20 percent of candidates; includes 80 percent of the jobs

Where are your chances better of getting the job you want?

| EXHIBIT 3.1 | The job market |

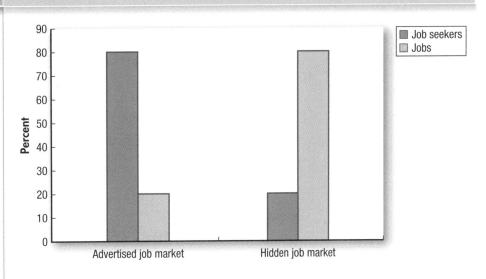

ARRANGE INFORMATIONAL INTERVIEWS

Informational interviews are defined as non–job-seeking interviews set up by job seekers in order to learn more about a certain position, company, or industry or to increase your network contacts. A related goal is to establish a contact, perhaps even a mentor, in a company who can help you with future networking and job-search endeavours.

Ideally, informational interviewing should take place before you begin your job-search interviewing in earnest. The beauty of this type of interviewing/marketing method is that you can do it anytime—and you should! Tap into your existing network to see if any individuals you already know might know someone who could help you with making contacts.

While using your existing network is an excellent way to make new contacts, you may not always find that it meets your needs. You may also contact the company you are interested in directly and ask for the proper contact or individual. Talk to the person about setting up a mutually convenient time for the interview. Job seekers are often concerned about contacting people they do not know, but are usually surprised by how agreeable most people are to conducting this type of interview.

Finally, informational interviews do not need to be stressful because there is no immediate job to be awarded. Also, many people are flattered when others come to them with questions or ask for advice, and many of these people willingly help out. You should research the company ahead of time so you will be more knowledgeable in your conversation. So, don't forget to use informational interviews early and often as a way to market yourself, acquire valuable help, and even as a good practice environment for the real thing—the job interview later on. Since the main focus in conducting informational interviews is to expand your network contacts, it is very important always to ask for additional contact names, either within the same company or externally. Follow up on the interview with a brief but formal thank-you letter.

Here are some typical questions you might find useful for informational interviewing. You may come up with more on your own that are more relevant to your career or the information you wish to secure. You must avoid asking questions that are too personal, such as questions about the salary or career direction of the person you are interviewing.

1. Can you describe a typical day in your position?
2. What do you like best and least about your job?
3. What steps did you take to gain this position?
4. What are the most prominent skills used in this position?
5. What is a typical career path for someone in your job?
6. What is your work environment like in terms of pressure? Deadlines? Routine assignments and activities?
7. If you could, what are some things you would change about your job or the company?
8. What advice would you give to someone like myself interested in pursuing a career in this industry?
9. How would you describe the work environment (atmosphere, culture, etc.) of your organization?
10. How is the economy affecting your organization?
11. What are the typical entry-level positions and job functions in your organization?
12. What qualifications does your company look for when hiring?
13. How important are grades/G.P.A. when your organization is hiring?
14. Who does your company hire (co-op students, recent graduates, etc.)?
15. Can you refer me to someone else who can provide me with further information?

MY Focus

There are two very useful methods of self-promotion. One is the old-fashioned technique of telling two friends about yourself and your job search and asking them to tell two friends, and so forth. In addition to just asking people to tell others that you are in the job market, send along copies of your resumé or personal business cards that show your degree or experience areas and how you can be reached. Marketing yourself in this manner builds a substantial network in no time!

The second is developing a 30-second script of self-introduction to use whenever you are with a potential networking individual. A template for developing your own script and sample introductions is available on the **Companion Website**.

MY Focus ESPECIALLY FOR COLLEGE STUDENTS

Many college students believe that the only time they should think about their future careers is during or at the end of their senior year. That's too late! There are some techniques that will lead to better self-awareness and self-promotion that you can, and should, be using right now! Check them out and get started.

■ Make an appointment to talk to your campus career advisor. Don't wait until the last minute to do this.

■ Check out newsletters and other publications in your placement or career services office and attend job-search workshops or other seminars.

■ Write or update your resumé and have it evaluated by the staff in the career services office or a trusted faculty member.

■ Collect information on cooperative education programs (co-op), internships, and other opportunities for part-time work that relate to your future career goal.

■ Consider volunteer positions (either in your field or in charitable or philanthropic organizations) that you can list on your resumé.

■ Subscribe to or check out from your school's library some of the professional journals in your chosen career field.

■ Join student chapters of professional associations on your campus or in the community and become active in programs and in networking with association members.

■ Join organizations that offer you diversity in activities and opportunities for future leadership roles.

■ Arrange to shadow someone in your field to learn more about the position, the company, and the industry. Your career services office may be able to supply contacts with alumni.

USE ELECTRONIC MARKETING

How can you use e-mail and the Internet to help with self-promotion? Use your imagination as you consider ways this technology can assist you. The Internet is global, so you have the world at your fingertips! Interested in talking to the head of a company or a department manager about their organization? Do some research and contact these people directly (if possible), or arrange an interview (either in person or by telephone) through their public relations office or the company's website. Many in management are willing to share their knowledge and wisdom with people just starting out.

Check the Internet for web groups, blogs, or discussion boards that include people in your career interest areas. Sometimes these sites can provide some great insider information. Don't forget to find out whether your college or university has its own alumni web board as well. Professional associations usually have a website, and many have student memberships. You may be able to attend an association's meetings or conferences, post questions or comments to online discussions, or even use the site's information to begin networking with other members. Join and participate in the organizations that interest you.

A Note of Caution

The list of job and career resources on the Internet grows every day. It can be exciting, exhilarating, amusing, confusing, exhausting. In any event, it can be time-consuming and perhaps addictive. A note of caution is probably a good idea at this point. It might be best to think of the Internet as a huge library that gives you access to materials and services from a wide range of sources. Evaluate those sources and services. Do they have a history of producing accurate and trustworthy information? Are they designed to help you? Are there fees involved? You may find that many sources and service agencies fit your needs, but you simply don't have the time to read or use them all. Be selective, and use your time wisely. Your career centre at your college or university often will have a list of good resources to use. Also, talk to other job seekers and share information about good sites. There are so many of them, and so many that come and go, that keeping current is a real challenge in itself. My advice is usually to stick with the main ones, along with the specialty ones for your career type and geographical area.

Internet and E-mail Etiquette

With job-search sites and job applications becoming so prevalent on the Internet and through e-mail, there are some major pitfalls that you can fall into if you're not careful. Chat rooms and e-mail have created their own lingo, which is seeping into other areas of life. You need to fully understand that it is not acceptable to use this lingo in the business world. This means in your everyday writing, e-mailing, and job applications.

When you e-mail a company to inquire about potential opportunities, you need to communicate in a businesslike manner. If you don't, you may be ignored. Don't waste time asking questions that may already be answered on the website. Your e-mail should be short and to the point, using these elements:

- Proper sentence structure
- Your full name
- Contact information
- Proper e-mail name (not hotlover@hotmail.com)

- Spell/grammar check
- No use of Internet/chat room slang
- Attachments must be able to be viewed by the reader
- Attach only properly named documents (not myresume.doc but rather Richard_Chan_Resume.doc).

When you apply to a company through e-mail, the common practice is to use the e-mail as a short note to notify the recipient that you are applying for a position. Let the recipient know that you are attaching documents, how many you are attaching, and the format they're in, as well as providing proper name and contact information in a signature line.

You then attach your cover letter and resume. Make sure you give them file names that will make sense when saved on the other person's computer, such as JohnSmithResume.doc.

When applying online at either the company website or employment sites, follow the application instructions closely. On some sites you will be able to upload your documents directly from your computer, while on other sites you may have to copy and paste your document. In case of the latter situation you should have your cover letter and resume ready in a text format. Often there will be a number of questions if it is an employer site. Read this information carefully and answer all of the questions.

These are often weeding-out questions. If you don't answer them correctly, your resume will not be forwarded to the proper person. Take your time. Watch for deadlines, because after the deadline your resume will not be processed.

DETERMINE THE BEST APPROACH

What is the best way to sell yourself? The best way to compete in any tough job market is to be *proactive* rather than *reactive*. *Proactive* means acting in advance—taking anticipatory action. *Reactive* is acting in response to something else. How do these two terms relate to self-marketing?

To market yourself well, you must take control. Make the first contact, spread the word, go after what you want, call the shots. Proactive candidates use the phone to make contacts and follow-up calls. They talk to people in person to network or follow up on leads. They are willing to go after what they want, knowing that in today's marketplace they can't wait around for the job to come to them!

Unfortunately, many people entering the job market are either unwilling or uncomfortable being proactive. These are the individuals who wait around for an employer to call or rely on other people to get interviews for them. These people only act in response to something or someone else. This approach takes the control and overall effectiveness of a job search away from them. They are passive and unmotivated, and they stay unemployed longer.

DEVELOP A POSITIVE ATTITUDE

Attitude is everything. What is the right kind? Well, the right kind of attitude for a job search is to be willing to undertake the job-search process. That may sound strange, but there are some who say they want to get good jobs, but when the hard work begins, they don't follow through. These people have cultivated a negative attitude. If you want to get a good job, but are unwilling to do the work it takes, you are ensuring that you won't meet your goal. Negative thoughts lead to negative actions.

Thinking negatively prevents you from getting the things you want. To change negative thinking, you must recognize it, remove it, and replace it with a positive attitude. Sustaining positive thoughts is the only way you can gain the success you want. For example, when a person says, "There is no job out there for me" or "I'll never get the job I need," he has ensured that he and the good job he is seeking will never meet. This person has paralyzed himself—he can't really go after what he wants because his thoughts are keeping him from it. His thinking becomes his reality.

On the other hand, if you continually play a positive tune in your head, one that tells you that you are worthwhile and helps give you confidence, you are bound to make that thinking a reality. So, when you are tempted to become negative, change your thoughts—substitute thinking that will help you believe in yourself. Replace "There's no job for me" with "This may be a pretty tough market, but I have the qualifications and skills that employers need. I am confident the position I want is out there, and I'm going to find it." That's developing a positive attitude.

There is a job-search book called *Your Attitude Is Showing.** Interesting name for a job-search book, right? This book's theory is that you must have a positive attitude before, during, and after the job search if you are to succeed. For example, your attitude is showing when you attend a career fair, when you answer interview questions, and when you network with people. Your attitude is "on" all of the time! So, you must have positive thoughts and positive actions if you are to win the job-search game.

USE A SYSTEMATIC STRATEGY TO PURSUE COMPANIES

The final suggestion in the selling strategies discussion is to use an organized method to go after the job you want. Before you can develop a strategic plan for contacting companies, you must have a personal plan with very specific goals and desired outcomes. The first step is to define your long-term or career goal. Next, determine what intermediate goals must be met in order to achieve that career goal. Finally, identify the short-term daily or weekly goals that must be accomplished to match the intermediate goals. Additional discussion and a Personal Goal Strategy are on the **Companion Website**.

Now, let's look at the details of a strategic plan for companies. How many companies should you contact? 10? 25? 50? The answer is that you should contact as many as possible. The more you advertise, the more likely you are to make the sale. Let's say you decide to contact 40 companies; how in the world can you do this short of hiring a staff and opening a campaign headquarters? The way to successfully market yourself to as many firms as possible is to use a strategic plan. The following demonstrates how a typical plan works.

You want to contact 40 companies, but you don't have time to call each one. How do you manage? Begin by prioritizing the companies into an A list, B list, and C list. Your A list includes the companies that you *really* want to work for, including your all-time dream company. Your B list has the companies that are also very attractive to you, but these firms are not your top 10. Your C list is composed of companies you would work for, those you have some interest in, but which you do not want to spend a great amount of time pursuing. For each company, list the name, address, phone and fax numbers,

---

* *Your Attitude Is Showing*, by Chapman & O'Neil, copyright © 2001 by Prentice Hall.

website and e-mail address(es). Include the names or position titles of people to contact, if possible. Consider the following as you develop your lists.

The A List

Think about the most effective ways for you to reach those firms you'd most like to work for. Perhaps you will call first for informational interviews or contact recruiters to set up interviews. Follow up any efforts with personal phone calls. Ask individuals to review your resumé, then send a copy with a cover letter to each firm. Follow up with letters or calls. Determine which companies will be involved in career fairs in the near future, talk to hiring authorities about current or future openings. These are your best job prospects and you should devote as much time and energy as you can to them.

The B List

Now, let's look at the second list. This list includes companies that are good prospects but are not ones you will pursue with the same intensity as those on the first list. You might send your resumé, check to see whether these firms will be interviewing in your area soon, or call some of the hiring authorities. For some companies on this list, you may want to follow up your resumé with a quick call to the firm's human resources department.

The C List

Companies on the C list are still ones you are interested in, and they'll be good practice companies if you're uncomfortable with your job-search skills. These companies will be an excellent starting point for you. Often when you start a job search you are not as confident in yourself as you would like to be. This is a good chance to develop your skills on companies you are less interested in. You can develop your ability to cold call, to follow up, to overcome objections, etc.

Today's job searches are challenging. More candidates are competing for fewer jobs. More media are involved in job searches—from newspapers to the Internet. At the same time you are conducting this sophisticated search, you are attending to your usual responsibilities, whether they be finishing college, working, or taking care of a family. You *must* have a plan for your search. A well-thought-out job-search strategy is not a luxury, it is a necessity! On the **Companion Website** is a template for creating your own A, B, and C lists. Complete the lists and your strategy for going after these companies to create a dynamic strategic plan.

INTERNET SOURCES

Of all the electronic sources at our command today, the Internet is the fastest-growing research tool. Its potential is truly amazing.

Note: Sites on the Internet change constantly. Therefore, some of the locations mentioned below may have relocated to different addresses or may have disappeared by the time you read this. Also, the listing of Internet sites in this book in no way indicates recommendation or endorsement by the authors or the publisher. These references are informational only.

Job Futures:
www.jobfutures.ca

Media Corp:

www.mediacorp2.com

Workopolis:

www.workopolis.com

Canada Jobs:

www.canadajobs.com

Human Resources and Social Development Canada:

www.hrsdc.gc.ca

Monster.ca:

www.monster.ca

Quintessential Careers:

www.quintcareers.com

Wow Jobs:

www.wowjobs.ca

Job Postings:

www.jobpostings.ca

FINDING YOUR FOCUS

1. Why is it important to learn about and use the hidden job market? How will you plug into it?

2. What are some specific ways you can use the Internet as an electronic means of marketing (other than resumé submission)?

3. How will you stay positive during your job search? Who can help you?

4. Name several of the A list, B list, and C list companies you plan to pursue in your job search.

5. List potential people/companies with whom you would like to conduct informational interviews.

4

Marketing Techniques

CHAPTER OBJECTIVES

After completing this chapter, you will be able to:

- Demonstrate the importance of networking in self-marketing, and use typical networking methods.

- Explain the role that telemarketing plays in personal networking, and use standard telemarketing techniques.

- Realize the importance of career fairs as a method of personal marketing, and fully participate in area career fairs.

Spreading the Word

If opportunity doesn't knock, build a door.

—MILTON BERLE

Now is a good time to point out the differences between marketing strategies and marketing techniques. The previous chapter on strategies discussed methods used to market yourself, such as informational interviews, electronic sources, and strategic plans for companies, as well as the importance of attitude. This chapter covers the most popular marketing techniques: networking, telemarketing, and career fairs. Because these three techniques are so effective, they are often called "the fast tracks to employment."

How do you find out about job openings? Where is the best place to look? The breakdown of how jobs are acquired looks something like Exhibit 4.1.

What does this say about the most effective way to learn where the jobs are? Although you should put some effort into answering "help wanted" or classified ads, conducting mass mailings, and even using the services of search firms, the most effective way to learn about job openings is through networking—all kinds of it. This chapter discusses just what is meant by networking, and outlines three important ways to contact those who know about job openings: personal networking, telemarketing, and career fairs.

NETWORKING

Networking is defined as developing and keeping relationships with others. It involves staying connected to people to learn about such things as new ideas, services, advancements, and, of course, job openings. Networking is most successful when done consistently over time. When it works, networking can "net" many gains for you personally and in your job search. Important aspects of networking include how to go about it, plan development, sample questions to use when talking to people about positions, and some networking do's and don'ts.

How to Go about It

"But I don't really know anyone; how can I network?" This is a common concern among those who realize the importance of networking but really aren't sure how to go about it. Everyone knows someone, and that someone knows someone else. Just as computers are linked to one another to share information, people have always been connected in some way. The most obvious people who have a prominent place in your network are immediate family members. Next come your friends, associates, classmates, professional people such as doctors or lawyers, members of associations to which you belong, and even your former coach or your children's coach.

EXHIBIT 4.1   **How jobs are acquired**

You must consider everyone you meet as a potential contact. The person who cuts your hair, the counter person at the deli or coffee shop, everyone! To help you explore just how many individuals you really do have in your network, complete the Network Planning Sheet below. Remember, you are listing people in your life who know other people, who know others, and so on.

Network Planning Sheet

Use this list to identify people who will become your first level of contact. It can be an effective starting point for your expanding network of people.

Family Members

Parents ———————————————————————————————

In-laws ———————————————————————————————

Sisters ———————————————————————————————

Brothers ———————————————————————————————

Others ———————————————————————————————

Contacts from Previous and Current Jobs

Employers ———————————————————————————————

Co-workers _____

Customers _____

Clients _____

Competitors _____

Others _____

Contacts from School

Administrators _____

Professors and teachers _____

Alumni _____

Classmates _____

Sorority/fraternity members _____

Others _____

Contacts from Religious Organizations

Clergy _____

Religious community leaders _____

Others _____

Contacts from Leisure Activities and Hobbies

Club members _____

Card/game groups _____

Physical fitness club members _____

Sports team members _____

Others _____

Contacts from Having Children

School administrators _____

Teachers _____

Parents of child's friends/classmates _____

Parents in carpool _____

School coaches _____

Parent–teacher association members _____

Parents in school-sponsored groups (Boy Scouts, Girl Guides, etc.) _____

Others _____

People I Know from the Past

Neighbours _____

Friends _____

Customers and clients _____

Former employees _____

Others _____

People I Know from Public Service and Charitable Organizations

Community fund _____

Chamber of commerce _____

Local government groups/committees _____

Environmental groups _____

Public safety groups _____

Service clubs (Jaycees, Rotary, etc.) _____

Other volunteer groups _____

Professional People I Know Who Know a Lot More People

Doctors and dentists _____

Accountant _____

Banker or financial advisor _____

Insurance agent _____

Hairdresser/barber _____

Mechanic _____

Other repair personnel _____

Developing a Plan

Now that you've determined the people to include in your network, you must devise a plan or schedule for contacting them. Where and how can you do this? As you are sitting in the hairdresser's chair, the accountant's office, or the grade school auditorium during the Christmas program, start a conversation with some of these people about your job search. Sometimes, opportunities to network arise during idle conversation; for example, your hairdresser asks you about your plans after college or your child's friend's parent asks you what line of work you are in. These are perfect opportunities to develop the conversation and include a statement about your current career goals. Following are some examples of such statements.

Hairdresser: "Well, Bill, what are you planning to do after graduation in June?"

Job seeker: "After graduation, I hope to become a web page designer for a small- to medium-size company. Do you know any web page designers or anyone who is involved in web page design?"

* * * * *

Father of son's friend: "So, what do you do when you're not coaching T-ball?"

Job seeker: "Currently, I am in electronics sales. But I'm planning to make a career move and am interested in telecommunications. What line of work are you in?"

Father: "Actually, I work in the cellular communications industry. We're a pretty big operation."

Job seeker: "Really? What is your company's name? Who is the Human Resource Director there?"

In addition to bringing up your career goals in casual conversation, you can be more direct. A physician, a sister-in-law, or a minister may already be aware that you are looking for employment. Therefore, in these circumstances, all you have to do is initiate a conversation. Instead of just asking about any firm that is hiring, ask whether your contact has any acquaintances who are in your field of interest. For example, your dog's groomer may have another client who has a sister who works for a software company. Or, you may have an uncle who serves on the town's water commission with a woman whose daughter works for a major insurance firm that is looking for a web page designer. The key is to "spread the word." Ask questions, strike up conversations, and ask your contacts if they know of other potential contacts. This type of personal networking is efficient and effective. Try it!

Before you get started, you need to think a bit more about your approach. Often people without a job think of themselves as unemployed. This can be a critical error. Think about the word. It is negative. It doesn't give others a reason to want to help you because it is totally passive. Starting now, you must change the way you think about yourself. You are actively "looking for employment." If you identify yourself in this way to people it gives them permission to assist you. It also makes it necessary for you to develop your plan and proceed with your networking and your job search.

There are some basic questions to have in mind in any networking circumstance, especially questions to ask people who have been referred to you by others.

Basic Questions to Ask Referrals

- Do you know anybody who might have or know of a job opening in my field?
- Can you refer me to someone who knows a number of people in my field?

Basic Questions to Ask a Contact Who You Don't Know

- How did you obtain your position or get into this field?
- What do you like (or dislike) the most about your job?
- Do you have any suggestions on how a person with my qualifications and skills might find a job in this field?
- What trends do you see in this field or how does the future look in this field?

Consider everyone you know or meet as potential contacts. Look for things you have in common with each person. Develop and use a short career goal statement that you can easily share with people. It's probably also a good idea to carry extra resumés or networking cards with you. You never know when they may prove handy to have. Keep some extras in your briefcase or in the car! And remember, 70 percent of all positions are found through networking. It is challenging work, but it does pay off handsomely.

Networking Cards

While you're looking for a job, you'll want to take advantage of every opportunity to build your network. Another technique for doing this is to create a networking business card for yourself. You can easily do this on a computer by picking up some blank business card stock from your local office supply store.

On the card you will have your name, address, phone number, e-mail address, website address, degree or diploma, and several key words that identify your top skills. You will always keep these cards with you, and whenever you meet someone you'll give him or her a card. This is an excellent way to start a conversation and increase your network of contacts. Don't be afraid to ask each person for new contacts that may be able to assist you. Remember—one of the key aims of networking is gaining additional contacts from current contacts. Using the name of the current contact makes it much easier to speak to the new contact.

The box below lists some of the dos and don'ts of networking. These hints are adapted from the book *Networking* by Mary Scott Welch.

EXHIBIT 4.2   **Sample networking card**

JONATHON SANDERS
645 Main St., London ON N2L 3H5
519 242 1047
jsanders@internet.ca

Hospitality Management Diploma
Customer Service◆Front Desk◆Bartending◆Serving Experience
Excellent Microsoft Office & Computer Skills
Smart Serve Certified◆Valid CPR◆French Bilingual

Networking Do's and Don'ts:

1. Try to give as much as you get from your network.
2. Keep contacts informed of your job-search progress, and keep in touch with your network over time.
3. Follow up on any leads or names you have been given.
4. Be professional in your approach and behaviour.
5. Continue to expand your circle of contacts.
6. Be clear about what you are looking for when making contacts.
7. Include people of all ages and job descriptions in your network.
8. Don't be afraid to ask for advice and assistance.
9. Don't expect your network to function as a job search firm for you.
10. Don't be discouraged if someone doesn't have time for you.
11. Don't be shy; speak out and be assertive.
12. Don't pass up any opportunities to develop your network.

TELEMARKETING

We've discussed why networking is so important to your job search and made some suggestions about those people to include in your network and how to contact them. As well as in-person the telephone is also an integral part of a successful job search.

How many ways can the telephone be used in your job search? For what purposes might you call someone? If you reflect on this question for a few minutes, you will discover that there are many ways the telephone can and should be used during a job search: to do your networking, seek information, answer a classified ad, follow up on a mailed resumé, follow up on an interview, contact references, follow up on leads received from contacts, thank contacts, thank references, and call family and friends to tell them that you got a job!

Telemarketing Guidelines

Using the Phone to Your Advantage

- Contact many employers in a short amount of time.

- Get information faster and more easily than with conventional mail.

- Contact the person doing the hiring.

- Obtain information so you will be more comfortable when it's time for the interview.

- Communicate your personality; you'll be more than just a name on a resumé, or a signature on a letter.

- Save money and time (and none of us has enough of these!).

At this point, you may be asking yourself, "Just how do I call people? What do I say? What if someone hangs up on me?" These are very good questions. Keep in mind that calling a potential employer not only saves you time, but also gets people's attention. Because everyone is busy (including you) and can't waste time on the phone, you must list the companies you want to contact, plan your calls, write down the key points you want to cover, practise your plan, and be willing to follow up and follow through. Following are some important guidelines to successful telemarketing.

List Companies

Before you let your fingers do the walking, do your homework. Make a list of the companies where you would like to work (use the A, B, and C lists you developed in Chapter 3). Ask people you know for suggestions and phone numbers; use the Internet, Yellow Pages, and reference books or directories.

Plan Your Calls

Good planning pays off when using the telephone. When is the best time to try to reach businesspeople? 8:00 a.m.? 12:30 p.m.? 5:00 p.m.? To some degree, the old rule of not calling at the beginning, middle, or end of the day doesn't apply anymore. In this era of non-traditional or flexible hours, many people have rather unusual work schedules. However, you should still try to stay away from the first hour or so of the workday. Would you want job seekers calling you at that time? The midday may not be an effective time to call either. Again, with varying hours, people may be taking lunch anytime between about 11:00 a.m. and 2:00 p.m.

So, when *is* the best time to call? Typically, 10:00 a.m. or 3:00 p.m. are good times. If that isn't always convenient for you, call during other times—it's better than not calling at all. Be careful about calling early Monday morning and late Friday afternoon if you can avoid it. The very worst times to call are at 8:00 a.m. on Monday or 5:00 p.m. on Friday! However, there are some who feel that calling very early or late may just find the hiring authority at her desk working alone.

Write Down What You Want to Say

When contacting a company, you don't want to forget anything important, and you want to be as confident as you can. Therefore, it is a good idea to write down what you want to say. Some believe a script is appropriate; others feel that just the key points are necessary. It doesn't really matter; do what's most comfortable for you. However, if you do use a script, don't read it word for word or sound like you memorized it. A potential employer wants to know three things about you right away: who you are, why you are calling, and what you can do for him. Outline your answers to these and any other related questions. Remember, you only have a short time to get your message across.

Practise

Before making your first calls, practise. After completing your script or outline, say the ideas out loud in complete sentences. Listen to your words and how your voice sounds. Do you sound professional and confident? Next, practise with a friend. Call her and role-play being a job seeker and an employer. Ask for feedback and adjust your message if necessary. You can also audiotape yourself to hear how you actually sound over the phone.

Follow Up and Follow Through

If you are fortunate enough to make an appointment with someone you have contacted, be sure to confirm the appointment as it draws near. If you reach message machines or voice mail, be patient. Call back at a different time. Don't bother to leave a message; you want to speak to people directly. If you keep getting a person's secretary, keep trying. Always be courteous to receptionists, secretaries, and assistants. These people often decide who gets to talk to their bosses and who doesn't!

Initiating Contact

Calling strangers without some type of referral can be a very scary prospect. How do you ask for the person you should talk to? Here are examples of how you might initiate contact:

- *"May I speak to the person in charge of your communications department?"*
- *"I would like to speak to the supervisor of your field technicians."*
- *"May I please speak to the manager of your engineering department?"*
- *"I am interested in speaking to the person in charge of your public relations department. Who is that?"*

You may also call a company and tell the receptionist that you have some correspondence (your resumé) to send to the head of the communications

department, engineering department, and so forth. Ask for that person's full name and address. Then, wait a few minutes, call back, and ask for that person by name.

If a secretary answers when you call, and that person asks what your call is in regard to, just say you have to discuss (or follow up on) some correspondence (resumé) or make an appointment (interview). You may even say that you have a business matter to discuss. Don't ever consider saying that your call is personal; that's dishonest and won't get you anywhere.

One last tip regarding your telephone requests: When you do reach the hiring authority and introduce yourself, it's best to ask for an appointment, not a job interview. If you are requesting an informational interview, ask for only 15 or 20 minutes. If your contact is considering whether to meet you, try asking, "Is a Tuesday or Wednesday better?" or "Before or after lunch?" When busy people are asked questions like these, they often respond automatically (i.e., "Wednesday is better" or "Before lunch is more convenient"). Then you are on your way to finalizing a meeting. Before making your telephone calls, review the following list of dos and don'ts.

Telephone Do's

- Prepare yourself before calling.
- Practise telephoning with a friend.
- Set up a daily plan.
- Keep pen and paper handy for notes.
- Keep a log of your activities.
- Turn objections around.
- Keep a smile on your face.
- Time your call carefully.

Telephone Don'ts

- Drink a beverage, chew gum, or smoke.
- Allow background distractions or noises.
- Sound as if you're reading a script.
- Speak too softly.
- Talk too technically.
- Rush through your presentation.
- Interrupt your contact.
- Act as if your contact can't see you.
- Be overbearing.
- Leave a message.

Sample Calling Script

Before looking at how to meet objections you may encounter when telemarketing yourself, let's review a sample calling script. This particular script ends with a positive response from the hiring authority. Even though you may not always get such a positive response, the script is a helpful model for your own telephone calls. Remember, it is all right to talk to someone in the personnel department about current or future openings, but the person you really want to speak to is the particular hiring authority for the specific position you are seeking.

Sample Calling Script

Switchboard: "Acorn Cellular. May I direct your call?"

Caller: "Yes, could you please tell me who hires the field service engineers at Acorn Cellular?"

Switchboard: "I believe that is Mrs. Creighton in personnel."

Caller: "I'd rather speak to someone in the field service department. Do you know who the manager is?"

Switchboard: "Well, that would be Mr. Kinsie."

Caller: "May I please speak to Mr. Kinsie?"

Switchboard: "Yes, one moment and I'll connect you."

Mr. Kinsie: "Field Service Department. This is John Kinsie."

Caller: "Good afternoon, Mr. Kinsie. My name is Carol Curtis. I'm very interested in employment at Acorn Cellular and was wondering if you are in need of an experienced field engineer."

Mr. Kinsie: "Well, I really don't have any openings at this time. Are you representing someone?"

Caller: "No, I'm looking for a field engineering position for myself. Do you anticipate any future openings?"

Mr. Kinsie: "There's a possibility we might be promoting some of our field service staff in a few months. At that time, we might look at your qualifications."

Caller: "Thank you very much, Mr. Kinsie. I will e-mail my resumé right away. Again, my name is Carol Curtis. I really appreciate your time on the phone today."

Mr. Kinsie: "Sure, no problem. I'll expect your resumé."

Meeting Objections

Obviously, not all phone calls will be as smooth as the one in the script. For those times when you meet objections or rejections, you must have a plan for how to handle them. First, realize that the negative comments you may hear are not directed at you personally. Sure, they may say that they don't have any openings or that you do not have the right kind of experience or some other objection, but these are the responses they give to everyone, not just you. So, have a thick skin and don't take the negative responses to heart. Remember, the more "no"s you hear, the closer you are to hearing that inevitable "yes!"

One sure thing about calling businesspeople for information or appointments is that you will meet objections. It's natural. Don't be discouraged by them, and try to be persistent without being obnoxious. Try to get at least one thing from each call you make: some information, another contact, or an interview. Whatever your goal, there is a common communication technique for meeting objections. When met with an objection during a phone call, most people stop in their tracks, apologize, and back off or even hang up. That may be what you feel like doing, but don't do it. Instead, use the following technique (adapted from *Guerilla Tactics in the Job Market* by Tom Jackson).

How to Handle an Objection over the Phone

- **Listen to and try to understand the objection.** Don't pretend you didn't hear it or that it is untrue. Don't argue with the person making the objection. Be sure the other person knows that you did hear and understand the objection.
- **Respond to it with a positive statement.** Reply with a statement of benefit that can overcome the objection without denying it. Let the other person know that although their objection may be true, you still have something of value to offer.
- **Repeat your original request.**

Below are some examples of how this technique might work.

You: "Is it possible for us to meet next week?"

Contact: "I don't think so. You don't have the kind of experience we are looking for."

You: "Yes, that's probably right. However, I think that the experience I do have could be very valuable to you in several ways. If we could talk for 20 minutes, I could demonstrate what I mean, and how I feel I could contribute to your department. May I have 20 minutes of your time next Tuesday or Wednesday? I would like to stop by and discuss this with you further."

Contact: "Well, I can't talk to you today. I'm going out of town on a sales trip."

You: "Yes, I know you must be very busy. However, if you could find a few minutes to meet with me when you return, I think I can help your staff with sales incentives and motivational techniques. Please tell me when you will be returning so we might discuss this further."

Two very important parts of this process are to acknowledge that you heard the objection, and to respond with a positive statement. Don't overlook either of these important steps. To help you feel comfortable meeting objections on the telephone, use the practice script found on the **Companion Website**.

Cold Calls

A cold call is when you go directly to companies to apply for a position that has not been advertised. You will do this in person and hope that you get an opportunity to speak to the person who makes the hiring decisions. Your goal is to make a strong impression so that you will secure an interview. At the very least, if you can get some contacts who may be hiring, your time will have been well spent. This method will work best with smaller companies.

Often after a first cold call, you find yourself sitting in the parking lot, with resumé in hand, wondering how it was that you got there. You didn't make an impression at all—even though you had the script in your head. What happened? Reality took hold and you now realize you need to be more aggressive. For this reason you don't want to start with your A list employers. You need to plan this out and practise with employers who are at the bottom of your C list.

It is also important to think about the type of employers with whom cold calls will be most effective. Cold calling works best with small and some medium employers. You will not likely have much success with large companies where you would typically need to have an appointment.

Steps to an effective cold call:

- Ask for the appropriate person or the hiring manager; research ahead if possible.
- Have that 15-second intro ready when you walk in the door; shake hands, introduce yourself, tell them the key points quickly, grab their attention.
- Go alone.
- Dress in a businesslike manner.
- Have your resumé, portfolio, etc., ready to present.
- Be ready for them to tell you they are not hiring; overcome objections.
- Leave your resumé, tell them you will follow up—and do it.

Cold calls are not easy, but with some practice you will develop techniques that will work for you. You'll discover ways of overcoming objections, of getting to speak to the person who really counts. You'll be able to start anticipating

challenges you will encounter. As you go through this process, your confidence will improve and you'll find yourself ready to move forward from your C list to your A and B lists.

A bonus along the way is that you may get a job offer, and you may discover that the company should have been on your A list all along.

CAREER FAIRS

Career fairs are excellent opportunities to meet and greet a large number of potential employers at one time. Although there are fewer career fairs these days due to increased recruiting over the Internet, there is still no substitute for face-to-face marketing. By all means, take advantage of the Internet to market yourself and learn about companies; however, don't pass up the opportunity to meet someone, shake her hand, and explain what you have to offer her company.

Career fairs are usually formal gatherings of recruiters held at area hotels or large meeting facilities. Typically, career fairs are attended by many recruiters who have immediate openings to fill, as well as some recruiters who are there to publicize their companies and gather resumés for future openings. Regardless, career fair attendance is useful for any job seeker. Why? It gives you an opportunity to network personally and pass out many copies of your resumé. Fair attendance also improves your social communication and interviewing skills. At the same time, you may meet other job seekers who can become contacts for you.

Career fairs are usually advertised in the classified section of major newspapers, through mailings, and even through the Internet. Some ask a small admission fee, while most are free. Career fairs usually run from morning to night, allowing both the unemployed and currently employed to attend. Some fairs are specifically designed for job seekers in a certain discipline such as engineering, medicine, or sales. Also, some fair organizers focus their events on people with some experience rather than recent college graduates, who usually meet recruiters on their campuses. In any event, consider attending as many fairs as possible.

Some career fairs are not for the faint of heart. You must be willing to walk up to a booth, stick out your hand, and introduce yourself. You must give a concise career statement and talk to the recruiter about the company and the position. You must also answer questions about your skills, qualifications, and goals. And you must be willing to compete with a large number of people who are trying to do the same thing!

Sample Career Fair Conversations

Look at the following sample conversations and the career fair tips to give you an advantage when using this direct marketing method for your job search. Remember, nothing takes the place of speaking directly to a person about your education, skills, and talents. Use career fairs to your fullest advantage!

Candidate: "How do you do? I'm John Sutton. I'm happy to see a representative from Collin Systems here."

Recruiter: "Pleased to meet you, Mr. Sutton. Are you interested in our telecommunications coordinator position?"

Candidate: "Yes, I am! I am currently employed as a LAN administrator and am looking for greater challenge in a new position. Here's my resumé. You'll see I have a related degree and five solid years of experience in this field. I'm very interested in hearing more about your opening."

This example gives you an idea of how easy it is to approach a recruiter at a career fair. Be friendly, be natural, and be direct.

The following sample conversation might occur when a potential candidate, a student, attends a career fair to make contacts and get information rather than apply for a position.

> Student: "Hello, Mrs. Norausky, my name is Taylor Lawrence. Although I won't be graduating from college until June, I am interested in learning about career opportunities in hotel/motel management. Can you tell me about your organization?"

> Recruiter: "Why, certainly. Highsmith Incorporated is an international firm that owns hotels in 10 major cities across the United States and Canada. We are always interested in competent people trained in hospitality management. If you would like, you may take some of the literature on our organization that I have here."

> Student: "May I take one of your business cards in case I have a question later on?"

> Recruiter: "Help yourself. Good luck with your future career, Taylor."

Career Fair Attendance Tips

Even though career fairs may seem intimidating, remember, employers are there to meet you. That's why they came. Put on your best suit, smile, and get ready to start selling yourself! Following are some important tips on career fair attendance.

- Come dressed as you would for an interview (clothes, shoes, hair, jewellery). Don't be tempted to dress down because it is "only a career fair." First impressions count—no matter where they occur!

- Take copies of your resumé to distribute and a supply of your personal business cards if you have them. Depending on the fair size, you should have between 25 and 40 resumés. Make it a goal to distribute all of the resumés you take along!

- Take a pen and portfolio for note-taking and collecting materials. Don't take a bulky briefcase or backpack. Remember, you want to appear businesslike and professional at all times.

- Take a smile, a firm handshake, a positive attitude, and a lot of energy. All of these things are essential. Be up, be positive, and be confident!

- Find out in advance which employers will attend the fair and know something about the ones in which you are particularly interested—thoroughly research three to four of your top companies. Recruiters are impressed when candidates go out of their way to learn about their firms before they come to the fairs.

- Talk to every employer about immediate openings or networking opportunities. Of course, you should visit the tables or displays of firms that have positions you are qualified for, but don't forget to do other networking. For example, if you have a degree in accounting and are interested in payroll or auditing, visit the firm advertising for a computer programmer—firms doing technical recruiting also have an accounting or payroll department. This is one way to network and get more mileage out of your career fair attendance.

- Approach employers as an individual, not in a group. Although it is more comfortable to attend fairs with friends, make sure you split up. Recruiters want to talk to individuals, not packs.

- Take advantage of times that are less crowded; for example, noon or 5:30 p.m. But be careful you don't arrive near the end of the fair. Recruiters may be tired and just want to pack up their materials and go home!

- Look the recruiter in the eye and use a firm handshake. Listen carefully to what the recruiter has to say and don't be distracted by other things around you.

- Prepare a brief introductory statement about yourself that includes your name, degree or major, type of position you are looking for, experience, goals, skills, and talents. Tell the recruiter why you wanted to visit that company's table. To help you prepare the introductory statement, a 30-second script can be found on the **Companion Website**.

- Be prepared for an on-the-spot interview.

- Prepare insightful questions or comments for the recruiter. Maybe you recently read an article about the firm that generated some questions. You might say something about how the open position contributes to the overall goals of the company or its mission statement.

- Maintain your energy and enthusiasm.

- Take short breaks but don't break your momentum. If you have a cup of coffee or a bottle of water during your break, don't carry it around with you even if you see others doing it.

In addition to the tips for a successful career fair experience, there are two more issues to address: follow-up and current trends in career fairs.

Career Fair Follow-Up

Within a week of the fair, follow up with a letter to each recruiter you met. Your letter should include the following:

- A thank you for the information and the recruiter's time.

- A review of one or two of your primary qualifications, with a reference to your knowledge of the company.

- A request for an interview and a statement that you will follow up the letter with a phone call within a week or two.

Experts disagree on the use of e-mail to follow up fair contacts. Some believe it appears the candidate has not invested time in the follow-up. Others feel it is efficient because it saves time for the candidate and the recruiter yet achieves the same goals as a letter. The choice is yours. Very ambitious candidates may do both!

Current Career Fair Trends

The age of technology affects how business is conducted at career fairs. Although you should bring copies of your resumé to distribute at the fairs, be aware that with the advent of the Internet, many companies have websites to market themselves and handle recruitment processes. What does this mean to the career-fair candidate? Recruiters may tell you to go to the website (the web address may be printed on the recruiters' business cards) to learn more about the company. They may also tell you to submit your resumé online by attaching a file to an e-mail message or completing a form on their web page. How common is this practice? Although it's hard to gauge the percentage of firms currently doing this, more and more are moving to a paperless submission. So, don't be discouraged if a recruiter doesn't take your beautiful, well-crafted resumé. Distribute what you can in person, and when you get home from the fair, submit electronic resumés to the recruiters who requested them!

When you leave a career fair, make sure to take some things with you. Remember, you should get as much mileage as possible from every event you attend. When you leave a fair, you should have:

- The business card from each recruiter you met.
- Notes you took on the various organizations and your discussions.
- Materials from different booths and tables.
- Thoughtful ideas about just where you may fit into the employment field, as you realize the types of jobs you do and do not want to pursue.

Finally, you will take away from your job fair experiences those skills gained by talking to a variety of people about yourself. This valuable experience will serve you well at future career fairs and future employment interviews.

Keep your self-marketing skills fresh by making several phone calls a week and attending as many fairs as you can each month.

Virtual Job Fairs

Recently there have been a number of virtual or online job fairs, which are often connected to college or university career centres. The fair will be active for a period of time such as two weeks or a month. The company websites or job postings will be featured, and potential candidates can search for companies of interest and follow the application instructions on the website or posting. There is no face-to-face contact, but you can access these fairs 24/7.

Personal Branding

Personal branding is the latest in hot topics. Branding means simply that when you think of brand names such as Nike, Apple, IBM, Tim Hortons, and Starbucks, you form an immediate image in your head. Personal branding is no different. You first need to determine who you are and the image you wish to portray. You then need to ensure that everything about you—your resumé, cover letters, portfolio, Internet presence, job-search strategies, and personal presentation—fits your branding. This sounds like a lot but there is some excellent information available to assist you.

Dan Schawbel is the leading personal branding expert for Generation Y, (also known as the Millennial Generation). He is also the author of *Me 2.0: Build a Powerful Brand to Achieve Career Success*. I would recommend going to his website for further information and links.

http://danschawbel.com/index.htm

SOCIAL NETWORKING

Facebook, MySpace, Twitter, and LinkedIn are just a few of the social networking sites available today and by the time this text goes to print there will likely be many more. Many people use these sites for exactly the reasons they were intended: to connect to people that you know. We live in a fast-paced society where simply by sitting a few minutes at our computers we can catch up with friends and see what they did on the weekend, what their future plans are, what they had for supper, and their innermost thoughts with a click of the mouse. Students are often shocked and appalled at the suggestion that anyone would use these sites for anything other than their intended purpose—for example, for potential employers to check out the character and day-to-day activities of a possible hire. The debate is too long to go into here, but the bottom line is that employers are checking out your online presence before they hire you. You need to be very aware that this is happening and that there are real-life cases of people who have lost out on their dream job, or been fired for what they say and show online. Often it may not even be your own page that turns a potential employer off but that of a well-meaning friend, for example, who has posted her favourite party picture of you.

So, think about this: if you know that potential employers are looking for your online presence, can you turn that to your advantage? Can you create a positive blog about something career-related? Can you turn your Facebook account into a positive marketing tool so that an employer viewing your page would be pleased to offer you an interview, or the job?

GLOBAL JOB SEARCH

Many Canadians are interested in foreign job opportunities. International experience is an excellent way to increase your marketability to employers, particularly these days, when we keep hearing about the "global marketplace." There are a number of ways to get this experience. You should be cautioned that landing an offshore job does take time, research, and persistence. If you have never lived or worked in another country, you may want to start with a program that provides assistance through each step.

One of the easiest ways that students and new graduates can secure visas to work in other countries is through the Student Work Abroad Programme (SWAP). Most college and university career centres will have this organization's current program information. You can also find SWAP on the Internet, on the Travel Cuts website. While the program is not set up to provide the job for you, your travel arrangements, visas, and the first couple of nights in the foreign country can usually be arranged. Many of the countries have their own supports to assist you once you arrive. More information can be obtained at www.swap.ca and in the organization's brochure.

Be aware that getting work visas from some countries (even the US) may not be as easy as you think. Below are some websites with information to get you started. You'll still need to do more research on your own, as the information changes frequently.

Travel Cuts (SWAP):
www.travelcuts.com

Overseas Jobs:
www.overseasjobs.com

JobBank USA:
www.jobbankusa.com

Cruise Services International:
www.cruisedreamjob.com

Castaway Cruise & Resort Hiring Agency:
www.cast-a-way.com

Department of Foreign Affairs:
www.international.gc.ca

EuroGraduate:
www.eurograduate.com

IAESTE (International Association for the Exchange of Students for Technical Experience):
www.iaeste.org

Working Abroad:
www.workingabroad.com

MY Focus — ESPECIALLY FOR COLLEGE STUDENTS

Use these strategies, based on information in this chapter, in your personal self-marketing campaign.

- Using the Network Planning Sheet, begin to develop your personal networking list. Add three to five new contact names each week and continue a dialogue with most of the people on your list.

- Develop your own calling script modelled after those in the chapter. Call a relative or friend and practise your script. Next, call a company in which you have some interest and use the script.

- Look at newspapers, professional journals, or college bulletin boards for upcoming career fairs.

- Develop your own 30-second script, select a fair, and attend. After working the fair, critique your experience, noting areas where you might improve for the next fair. Then, try again! Always follow up with any recruiters with whom you had promising discussions.

FINDING YOUR FOCUS

1. List three or four way to create your personal job-search network.

2. Describe several advantages to using the telephone in your job search. What advantages do you plan to make the most of and why?

3. Describe the method for meeting objections on the telephone.

4. List companies you would be interested in cold calling.

5. Review the career fair tips. Which will be the most challenging for you, and how will you meet these challenges?

CHAPTER OBJECTIVES

After completing this chapter, you will be able to:

- Identify resumé types and decide which is best for you.

- Create several versions of your resumé that sell you to an employer and accommodate the ways in which resumés are transmitted.

- Adapt to the scannable resumé technology.

- Appreciate the importance of reference selection and use.

- Be aware of the questions your reference contacts may be asked.

- Create your own personal list of references.

Critical Tools for Success

Always think in terms of what the other person wants.

—JAMES VAN FLEET

Developing a resumé is an important part of your job search and is usually one of the first steps taken in the job search process. Revising your resumé is something you should do frequently during your career to reflect any changes in your professional life and to include any new skills you develop and experience you gain.

A resumé cannot get you a job; however, a good resumé can help you get to the interview stage. So, the goal of the resumé is to get the interview. With that in mind, a resumé should tell recruiters enough to make them eager to meet you, but not so much that they have no reason to talk to you in person. Also, your resumé should look appealing and be easy to read. Resumé writing can be challenging and requires considerable effort—the key is to achieve just the right mix of interesting content and engaging format.

Remember, your resumé will probably find itself in a pile or an inbox of several hundred. Most resumé readers spend only a minute or two on each resumé. What will make yours the one chosen for consideration? What will be the first information they read about you and how impressive will it be? When recruiters first look at your resumé, they don't spend a great deal of time scrutinizing every word. They initially look for those key traits, technical skills, and previous experiences that satisfy the requirements of the open position. Their eyes are drawn to industry buzzwords and quantified statements. For example, a quantified statement about managing a local area network might say that the candidate managed a network of 130 Dell computers, handling user complaints, upgrades, security, and routine maintenance.

Also keep in mind that your resumé may be read first by a computer. Resumé scanning software is discussed later in this chapter. Finally, because the resumé often serves as a springboard for questions and discussions during the interview, all information must be truthful, accurate, and easy to follow.

PREPARING TO WRITE YOUR RESUMÉ

As you can probably tell already, successful resumé writing is not just putting your education and work history down on a piece of paper. There are many issues that you must consider. This chapter first covers the following resumé aspects and addresses the important issues for successful resumé writing:

- resumé types
- resumé styles, including electronic resumés
- resumé sections
- resumé guidelines
- resumé tips

The second section provides samples of the main resumé types and formats. The last section of this chapter discusses selecting and using references.

TYPES OF RESUMÉS: CHRONOLOGICAL VS. FUNCTIONAL

There are two types of resumés: chronological and functional. You may also hear of a combination resumé, but that is really just a chronological resumé with more emphasis on your skills, qualifications, and key traits. There is a tendency among job seekers to create a chronological resumé because it is perceived as the easiest to write, and most resumé samples are this type. Keep in mind that you want the best type for your particular circumstances and job-search goals. So, think about the types and decide which represents you the best. All of the sample resumés discussed below can be found in the section "Resumé Samples" (Exhibits 5.1–5.6) beginning on page 69.

In the *chronological resumé* format (see Exhibit 5.1), information is organized according to time, listing the most recent education and experience first and working back to earlier education and experience. This is by far the most widely used type because of its simplicity. It is an appropriate format to use if you have had continuous employment and are interested in providing a historical view of your past. Chronological resumés focus on dates and individual job experiences. It is often the most suitable for students and recent graduates.

The *functional resumé* format (see Exhibit 5.2) organizes information according to types of experiences or functions. Rather than relying on dates and time frames as in the reverse chronological format, this format spotlights key traits or qualities, providing details and examples that demonstrate those qualities. This format requires a bit more thought and planning than the first; however, one of its strengths is that it is not like the majority of resumés—a fact that unfortunately can also be one of its main weaknesses.

This format is useful if you do not have continuous employment experience or if you want to focus the reader's attention on *what* you did rather than on *when* and *where* you did it. This resumé is also called an accomplishments or skills resumé. It allows you to reflect on the most prominent skills and qualities you bring to the career market, and provides a format for you to organize these skills and qualities in such a way that they become the focus of the resumé. It can be most useful for someone who is making a total career change. The functional resumé is often the best choice for the mature student with a new career focus.

Targeted Resumés

You may be hearing a lot about targeted resumés. Targeted resumés simply mean that they must be targeted toward your job objective and the position you are applying for. Industry key words and relevant skills are very important to highlight. Your resumé needs to be tweaked for every position you apply for.

Examples of Individuals Who Should Use Functional Resumés:

- Previous experience is line work in a factory. New career: office administration
- Previous experience is business, banking, and insurance. New career: technologist
- Previous experience is office administration. New career: nursing
- Previous experience homemaker, mother, and/or volunteer. Re-entering the workforce
- Previous experience labourer. New career: millwright apprentice

In addition, you also need to target your entire application through your cover letter, by highlighting the specific skills and qualifications the employer is looking for. Whether you choose to create a chronological or a functional resumé, it will not represent you well unless you tailor it for each position you are applying for.

Steps to Create a Targeted Resumé

- Highlight the qualifications, skills, experience, and qualities on the job description that you possess
- Create an objective on your resumé for the specific position and company
- Create proof statements to demonstrate the skills and qualifications that are relevant to the position
- Ensure your experience provides additional proof of the requirements for the position. You don't want to just list what you did in the position but target it towards what is relevant for the new position you are applying for
- Add any relevant volunteer activities and interests
- Review your references
- Review the posting again and ask yourself whether you have focused on and proven the most important aspects of the position

SECTIONS OF A RESUMÉ

Resumés are formatted using a number of essential components or resumé sections that employers will expect to see. They are discussed in detail below. While there are options in discussing resumé sections, you should always remember that your resumé is your sales tool and will work best for you if you provide the reader with all of the information he or she is looking for when deciding whether to interview you. Missing sections will look like an incomplete package to an employer.

Let's take a look at the various sections.

Heading

Your heading includes your name, address, phone number, and e-mail address. Students sometimes find it useful to list both current and permanent addresses so they can always be reached. In the past, job seekers included both home and work phone numbers when possible. With the popularity of cell phones, many candidates are listing just one number: their cell phone number. This is fine, but remember, your cell phone could ring at any moment with a recruiter on the other end. If you include your cell phone number on your resumé, be prepared either to respond to that call immediately or defer it to your voice mail for later handling. Always remember to use postal codes and area codes.

Include your e-mail address on your resumé. Listing an e-mail address says that you are comfortable with this communication technology and use it in your everyday life. Just a couple of words of common sense here about e-mail addresses. If your current e-mail address name is not as professional as it should be, change it before you start using the address on your resumé.

What about including your personal website? If you have a website, don't automatically list it in the heading. Consider whether you want it to be seen by a potential employer. Website references on resumés are particularly appropriate for individuals desiring positions as webmasters or web designers. But remember: any web page referenced in a resumé should be professional looking and in good taste.

Objective

An objective is a clear and concise statement of the type of job you are seeking. Be original, and avoid phrases such as "wish to gain experience" or "desire for advancement." Mention the specific position or career area you are interested in. Your objective should tell the recruiter the purpose of your resumé. The rest of your resumé should provide the proof that you are qualified for your objective. It should be short and to the point.

Not all experts agree on the importance of stating your objectives, but you want to ensure the reader knows what you are applying for. Remember, this objective is for your current resumé—not where you want to be in five years.

Personal/ Professional Summary

Instead of stating a career objective, some people include a personal or professional summary. This section may say more about you than a typical career objective statement. This section focuses on what you have accomplished and what technical or personal traits you have to offer. Reflect on your past positions and your accomplishments to create a personal or professional summary. Producing succinct statements about yourself and your qualifications impresses most resumé readers, who tend to pay closer attention to the material at the beginning of the resumé. This section tends to be used more often by professionals who are midway into their career.

Education

How prominently you wish to display your education and how detailed you choose to be depends on how long it has been since you were in school. Recent graduates, who will spotlight their education, should include grade point average and honours. If you have been in the workforce for a while, you may merely include your degree, school, and year of graduation. For those who have been in the workforce for some time, listing education on the resumé may not be necessary or it may be included lower down. To help you prepare an education section for your resumé, complete the following worksheet.

REPRESENTING EDUCATION ACTIVITY

This exercise is designed to help you think about aspects of your education. Answer the following questions to construct a complete educational and qualifications section for your resumé.

1. State the name of the educational institution you most recently attended. Include the city and province where the school is located.

_____

_____

_____

2. Give the correct name of the diploma/degree you are working to attain or have attained.

_____

_____

3. Supply the month and year of your graduation.

_____

4. Indicate your grade point average (for recent graduates).

_____

5. List any honours or academic achievements.

_____

_____

_____

6. List several of your favourite courses in which you did well.

_____

_____

_____

7. List those courses that involve the subject matter relating to the career you are pursuing.

_____

_____

_____

8. Decide what additional course work you want to mention in your resumé. Consider grouping courses into several categories with appropriate headings.

_____

_____

_____

9. Highlight any special equipment (computers or other types) on which you are proficient, and any software or computer languages you have learned in school or taught yourself.

_____

_____

10. List any other post–high school educational institutions attended. Give names and locations.

_____

_____

11. If you obtained a diploma/degree from the institutions listed in question 10, indicate the title and the date of graduation.

_____

_____

12. List any honours or special comments about the course work listed in question 10.

_____

_____

13. If your high school graduation was recent, you may discuss any special course work, honours, programs, or projects.

_____

_____

_____

Please note that most of this information will not go in your Education section, but will fit well in your Skills and Qualifications section if you have a chronological resumé, or in other sections if you have a functional resumé.

Skills and Qualifications

This section is a very important and useful part of the resumé. It should hold a prominent position in the resumé, even above the experience section. In this section you should highlight the important skills, certificates, and training that are relevant to your desired field of employment and your objective. Computer skills, languages, and special licenses and certificates should all be included here. You may also want to highlight some of your transferable skills. Using scope and achievement statements can help market this area well. You should be thinking about listing your relevant coursework here, but do not list the course names. Rather, think about the key skills that you developed from that course; think about the potential employer reading the resumé. The skill or competency is much more relevant than the course name.

Work Experience

When completing this section, provide job titles, company names, and the cities and provinces in which the companies are located. There is no need to include street addresses or the names of managers or other personnel. For each position, briefly describe your duties and responsibilities. When describing your previous and current jobs, use action verbs to demonstrate accomplishment. Simply listing duties and responsibilities is not enough for a superior resumé. For the best resumé possible, develop more insightful descriptions of your work experiences. Adding impact to your work experience is discussed later in this chapter.

How far back should you go when listing your employment history? That depends. The rule of thumb is five years; however, if you had some noteworthy experience previous to that time, you may include it as well. Certainly, if you have extensive work experience, you may want to include a greater number of previous positions.

For many, work experience is the most important section of the resumé. Unfortunately, this is also often the most poorly written section. Often job seekers merely create a list of work experiences by listing their duties. They miss the opportunity to grab the reader's attention with key ideas and specific accomplishments. All job seekers should know how to add impact to their work experience. The following discussion explains how to do this.

Adding Impact to Your Work Experience

To create a work experience section with more impact, include more in your job descriptions than simply the duties. Most resumé writers do a very good job of listing job responsibilities. The problem is, you are telling the reader what she already knows: salespeople deal with customers and handle accounts, secretaries create documents and schedule appointments, computer programmers program computers! Try thinking about your work experience a little differently. As you reflect on your duties, also think about the *scope of responsibilities* you have had and your *accomplishments on the job*. The box below shows two examples using the positions of computer programmer and sales representative.

See how this attention to scope and achievement in your job description is more powerful and more informative? Which person would you rather talk to: the salesperson who merely said he was in charge of outside sales or the person who said that she was responsible for a 30 percent increase in revenues over a six-month period? I think you get the idea. Don't despair if you don't have impressive achievements at this stage in your life. Just think about all aspects of your past and present employment, and determine how you can make your job experience section move beyond the mundane description of job duties by completing the work experience exercise that follows.

WORK EXPERIENCE EXERCISE

Directions

Before you develop the work experience section for your resumé, try this exercise. It provides an opportunity to think creatively about the jobs you've held.

Using the list of action verbs found on page 62 and your imagination, create some innovative job descriptions for the positions described in Situations 1–3 (starting on page 57). Pay special attention to the use of action verbs. Remember that a current job is described with phrases using present tense verbs; keep descriptions of your previous jobs in the past tense.

Highlighting Scope and Achievement

COMPUTER PROGRAMMER POSITION

Duty statement: Wrote code and performed troubleshooting using Visual Basic.

Scope statement: Worked as a member of a four-person project team to create code and solve programming problems in a PC-based environment.

Achievement statement: Wrote and maintained a computer program using Visual Basic that analyzed current work-flow operations, reduced analysis time by 50 percent, and served as a model program for six divisional offices.

SALES REPRESENTATIVE POSITION

Duty statement: Supervised outside sales for computer division.

Scope statement: Sold electronic components to 140 clients in a five-province region of Canada.

Achievement statement: Maintained successful five-province sales region of 140 clients, averaged five new accounts monthly, and generated a 30 percent increase in revenues over a six-month period.

Example

You worked at Carlson's Cafe for three years while attending college. Your title was assistant restaurant manager, and your responsibilities included managing a staff of 10 servers, scheduling your staff, taking care of any problems or disagreements that occurred with staff members or patrons, running the cash register, doing the banking, and training new servers as they were hired.

A creative job description for this example might include:

- Trained and managed a staff of 10 employees
- Handled staff scheduling
- Provided friendly and prompt customer service
- Operated and troubleshot problems with electronic cash register
- Balanced daily cash receipts
- Communicated with restaurant staff and owners to improve restaurant operations

See what you can do with the following situations. Don't forget to use those action verbs effectively!

Situation 1

You worked for several years as a technical writer for a software company. Your duties included converting programming notes into plain English for user documents. You created appropriate graphics using several desktop publishing programs, solicited printing quotes from local printers, and handled ordering and the distribution of manuals and documents. You also created marketing brochures for the sales staff, and occasionally helped with other company promotional programs.

Description #1

_____

_____

_____

_____

_____

_____

_____

Situation 2

You are the owner and manager of a daycare centre located in a mid-size town. You recruit and hire qualified daycare providers; manage the centre's day-to-day operations; handle provincial licensing and compensation paperwork; and plan, purchase, and prepare food for your staff and the children. In addition, you plan special interest programs in art, music, and physical education for the children. You are implementing a "Computers for Kids" program that will be a model for centres across the province.

Description #2

_____

_____

_____

_____

_____

_____

_____

Situation 3

You currently work as a telemarketer with minimal supervision. You are responsible for keeping accurate records of the calls you make as well as tracking the outcome of each call. You were named Employee of the Month when you organized a mini-workshop for your co-workers on how to handle difficult customers. Your supervisor sometimes calls upon you to substitute for her. You volunteer to work extra hours when co-workers are sick. You have consistently scored as one of the top two salespersons in your division.

Description #3

_____

_____

_____

_____

_____

_____

_____

Your Turn!

Using the job you currently hold (or the last one held), write a paragraph describing the position and the duties and tasks associated with it, then develop a creative job description suitable for inclusion in your resumé. Remember to use action verbs and the correct verb tense.

Job Title

_____

Situation

_____
_____
_____
_____
_____
_____
_____
_____

Description

_____
_____
_____
_____
_____
_____
_____
_____
_____
_____
_____
_____
_____
_____
_____
_____

Now, write a description for all of the positions you intend to put in your resumé. Don't be shy about any of your accomplishments.

Personal   This is a section that not all job-search experts agree on. If you have the space, you may want to include a line or two about some personal characteristics or activities. Sometimes, these comments help to make the person behind the resumé seem more real. At the same time, you must be careful not to mention anything in this section that could be controversial (e.g., politics, religion).

When you put these sections together to form your resumé, remember that the most important information must go first. Therefore, if you are experienced, your work section follows the heading. If you are a recent graduate, education is your most prominent section. If you include a personal section, it should be placed near or at the end of the resumé.

References

If space permits, you may choose to state that your references will be provided upon request. If you have little space remaining, omit this statement. Employers expect you to provide references regardless.

For more information on using references effectively, see the References section beginning on page 76.

CONVERTING YOUR RESUMÉ FROM CHRONOLOGICAL TO FUNCTIONAL

You have made the decision that your format and style are not working for you any longer, but where do you start? Don't try to convert your previous resumé. Start a brand new resumé. Look at the sample Functional Resumé 5.2.

Determine what direction your career is now taking. What are the skills that you will need to be successful in this career choice? Start with a list of your relevant transferable skills. Use the Transferable Skills Checklist in Chapter Two. This list should start out long; you will sort and add proof statements later.

Next, you need to determine your subtitles under the Skills and Qualifications section. Usually three or four titles are enough.

Sample Subtitles to Choose From in your Skills and Qualification Section:

- Technical
- Computer
- Communication
- Interpersonal
- Organizational
- Team Work
- Sales
- Marketing
- Customer Service
- Management
- Supervisory

Now you need to sort your transferable skills under your chosen subtitles (see Functional Resumé Example 5.2). Add scope and achievement statements and even the company name, in brackets, where you developed that skill. The scope and achievements exercise follows in this chapter.

This will take some revising. One of the most difficult parts of this exercise if you are changing careers is the feeling that you are leaving behind who you were. This is all about looking forward and presenting your previous skills in a manner that a future employer will utilize. If you don't do this well, they will pass you by.

You may need to get a second opinion and some guidance with this. Contact the Career Services department within your college or university. It may take two or three attempts to get it right but perseverance will pay off.

RESUMÉ GUIDELINES

These guidelines reiterate and emphasize some points already discussed.

The resumé is a sales tool, and as the salesperson you must use this tool effectively. It is crucial that your sales tool be the best it can be. To ensure this, pay particular attention to the content (what you say) and the layout (how you structure your content on the page). The format should be engaging and easy to read; your content should be impressive, interesting, and promotional in nature, as well as honest and accurate. An impressive resumé is a blend of good content and attractive format.

Your resumé should read easily and quickly. You may have only 10 to 15 seconds to attract the attention of the recruiter and encourage that person to read in more detail. Keep in mind that most of us read from the top of the page at the left margin down in a somewhat diagonal direction when we are trying to scan a document to get the greatest amount of information in the least amount of time.

Resumés are quickly scanned because recruiters receive hundreds of resumés each day. They literally don't have time to read each one word for word during the screening phase of their resumé review. Because recruiters have these time constraints, it is important for your best and most important information to be close to the top of the page and for your format to be inviting and easy to read.

When readers scan a resumé, their eyes will be drawn to specifics that relate to the positions they are looking to fill. Because of this, be sure to highlight any technical terms, buzzwords, or personal characteristics that recruiters may be looking for.

Resumé Length

While many sources recommend that your resumé should only be one page, this goal is often not realistic. The main focus of your resumé is to attract the attention of the potential employer. If your resumé is crowded onto one page, nothing will stand out. White space is an important component of the resumé. Do not be afraid to use a second page, but make sure that the most relevant information is on the first page. If you do use two pages, make sure you put a header with your name and phone number at the top of the second page.

Remember: A resumé is not designed to be a complete personal history. Rather, it is a specification sheet about a product (you) written in such a way that the recruiter will want to learn more from you in person during the interview.

Because recruiters need to review resumés quickly, it is not a good idea to include attachments to your resumé, such as grade transcripts or letters of recommendation, unless asked. This extra information is not as important at this preliminary step of the job-search process as it will be later on. Recruiters are concerned with seeing whether you look like a good candidate on paper. Thus, provide only the material that is relevant to this stage of the job-search process.

Resumé Writing Style

General writing style for a resumé is quite different from that used for a letter or a business report. Instead of using complete sentences and lengthy paragraphs, present information about yourself in as clear and concise a manner as possible. Remember, your resumé is a glimpse of you as a candidate for a particular position, not your life story! Use bulleted phrases that express complete ideas in a clear, concise manner.

Start new ideas or phrases on the left-hand side of the page whenever possible, and use bullets to make the lines of type easier to read quickly. To help sell yourself in your resumé, begin lines with action verbs. These are power words that grab the reader's attention and indicate what actions you have taken and what accomplishments you have. Action verbs are discussed in more detail below.

Resumé Accuracy

Is correctness that important? Yes! Your resumé needs to be accurate and correct. Do not estimate or approximate—be sure you are accurate with such things as titles, dates, and responsibilities. Today's recruiters are rather skeptical of what people put on their resumés, feeling there has been a growing tendency to lie or exaggerate what is being said. Make sure all details on your resumé are factual and accurate.

Using Action Verbs

To ensure a dynamic and powerful resumé, use action verbs to describe your school and work experiences. Read through the following list, circling the verbs that apply to your school and work activities. Then, use this list as you draft your resumé.

act/perform	direct	lead	report
adapt	distribute	learn	research
advise	enforce	listen	resolve
analyze	entertain	locate	restore
anticipate	estimate	log	retrieve
appraise	evaluate	maintain	review
arrange	examine	manage	run
assemble	exhibit	meet public	schedule
assess	expand	memorize	select
audit	explain	mentor	sell
budget	explore	motivate	service
calculate	find	negotiate	set
check	fix	observe	solve
collect	gather	obtain	sort
communicate	generate	operate	speak
compare	handle complaints	order	study
compile	handle equipment	organize	supervise
compute	handle money	perform	support
confront	help people	persuade	test
contact	illustrate	plan	teach
control	implement	prepare	train
coordinate	improve	process	translate
cope	inform	produce	troubleshoot
create	initiate	program	understand
decide	inspect	promote	update
delegate	install	protect	upgrade
deliver	instruct	question	verify
demonstrate	interpret	raise	volunteer
design	interview	read	work
determine	invent	reduce	write
develop	investigate	recommend	

WHAT IS AN ELECTRONIC RESUMÉ?

The term electronic resumé is used to describe resumés that are scanned by a computer and those that are posted on the Internet. Both are electronic and differ greatly from the traditional paper resumé. Resumés that are scanned into software programs by employers are very focused, basic, and rely on key traits to promote individuals. Resumés posted on the Internet tend to look like traditional resumés initially, but the reader may discover that he or she can travel to additional areas of the resumé through hypertext or links.

Let's look further at the scannable resumé. To understand what is needed in a scannable resumé, you must be familiar with the capabilities of this resumé-scanning technology.

Resumé-scanning software has been used by Fortune 500 companies as well as small firms for some time now. This software performs many functions, including resumé scanning and tracking. This specialized software can also generate response letters to applicants. In addition, some systems help firms track who has been hired and can store other personnel information in a human resources database.

How does resumé-scanning software work? As each resumé is scanned into a computer, the program looks for those key words identified by company personnel as important. For example, a department manager may have the database search for a candidate with certain accounting knowledge. In addition to the accounting key words that are programmed into the software for that particular position, some programs can identify desirable employee traits and place them in various categories such as "must have" or "important to have." Resumé software programs rank resumés according to the number of "hits" or "matches" between the key words listed and those appearing on a resumé. The next section discusses an example of how an employer might process an electronic resumé.

Processing an Electronic Resumé

Many employers process all incoming resumés electronically. Resumés are scanned as images and special software is used to read the text. The text is then entered into an electronic database. When an employer is ready to review the resumés, the employer searches the database for possible candidates by selecting appropriate key words. Resumés that match a specified score for the relevant key words are then selected and printed.

Because computers read resumés differently than people do, recruiters recommend that job hunters prepare at least two versions of their resumé, one for scanning and one for human readers. On an electronic resumé, key words can be listed in a separate key word section (see Exhibit 5.6) or integrated into the text. In general, action verbs like "managed" or "facilitated," which are highly recommended for use in paper resumés, are not effective in electronic resumés because most scanning software programs look more for noun key words than verbs.

Why do companies use these scanning programs? Mostly because they save time, energy, and money. A computer can scan and store a resumé in seconds and quickly retrieve it a year later if necessary. Scanning programs objectively review information on resumés. Some employers feel this technology enables them to respond more quickly to applicants than the more labour-intensive methods of the past. To help you determine which type of resumé is appropriate for a specific company, first call the company if possible to see if it uses scanning software. Research the company website to further aid you in your application process. No matter how you transmit your resumé initially, remember to take an attractive paper copy of it to the interview.

Be aware that advice on the techniques of good electronic resumé writing varies. Some resumé-scanning software has become sophisticated enough to handle such format elements as italics or underlining. Keep yourself informed of the latest technologies used in the job-search arena and revise your own methods accordingly.

Resumé Scanning Advice

TIPS ON FORMATTING

- Make sure your name is the first readable item and is on its own line.
- Use plain white paper measuring 8.5 by 11 inches.
- Use standard fonts such as Times New Roman, New Century Schoolbook, or Courier.
- Use standard 10- to 14-point font.
- Original should be laser printed.
- Don't use italics or underlining. (You may use boldface and capital letters for emphasis.)
- Don't use shading, boxes, borders, or graphics.
- Don't staple or fold the resumé.

TIPS TO MAXIMIZE HITS

- Have plenty of key words for the software to pick up.
- Focus on using nouns (name of degree, software names, department names, etc.) rather than verbs, as in a more traditional resumé.
- Use key words and industry jargon or buzzwords.
- Describe experience with concrete words, not vague ideas.
- Don't feel you must limit the resumé to one page.
- Use common headings found in traditional resumés.
- Consider including a cover letter identifying the position you are seeking.

Additional Guidelines for Using Scannable Resumés

The electronic era has ushered in new considerations and techniques for those wishing to compete for positions in the current electronic age. Gone are the days when you could just stuff a resumé into an envelope and mail it. Applicants must be aware of the latest technologies and methods of application.

If your resumé has been scanned, it is usually in that firm's permanent file. When following up on the disposition of your resumé, consider asking such questions as "Did you receive my resumé?" "Was I a match in your desired skill areas?" "Has my resumé been routed?" Some recruiters believe that the operative word for finding out if your resumé (and you) have made it to the next step of the screening process is "routed." If you follow the advice and recommendations discussed here and can demonstrate you are a good candidate for the position, you have a good chance of having your resumé routed to the right people in an organization. If you can achieve this, you are on your way to the next step in the job search process, the interview. Additional information and advice on scannable resumés is on the **Companion Website**.

No matter the type of resumé you create, you must do the best job possible for it to be an effective tool in your job-search campaign. It is easy to put together an average resumé. It takes some thinking and good writing to create a dynamic, outstanding, successful resumé. Be prepared for the commitment it takes to craft an outstanding resumé if you want to compete successfully in the job market.

As technologies change, this process has also changed a lot in the last year. When you upload your resumé to a website you will be faced with two different methods depending on the website. If the website has a browse feature to allow you to upload your resumé, the process is very straightforward and you simply have to attach your resumé as requested. This is the newer technology and works very well.

Many companies still use an online application template and require you to have a box and copy and paste a text (.txt) resumé. It is very important in these cases that you do not copy and paste your document directly without first converting it to a text-based document. Follow these steps below to convert.

- Open your resumé in Microsoft Word.
- Rename your resumé as something simple like Alan Wong Text Resumé, change the format to plain text (.txt) format, and resave.
- It will alert you to the fact that proceeding with this step will cause you to lose your formatting. Check OK.
- Open Notepad (found under Accessories).
- Open your newly saved resumé.
- You will notice that all of the formatting has been removed and likely your bullets have been replaced. This is what you want.
- Now modify it further by justifying everything to the left. Use spacing to separate sections. Take out all tabs. This resumé doesn't have to look nice, but it does have to be easily read by the employer. Take out any page numbers or second-page headers.
- Resave it and then copy and paste this version onto the website.

RESUMÉ TIPS

This section discusses a few tips to ensure the best possible resumé for your job search.

Personal Content

Stay away from mentioning anything personal that is not directly related to the job. This includes your age, date of birth, health status, and Social Insurance Number.

Paper Choice

While most resumés are now sent electronically, you will sometimes need a hard copy. If you plan to send resumés by regular mail, drop it off directly to the company, or print off a copy to take to the interview, the safe choice for paper colour is white. A beige, buff, or light grey colour can also be used. Avoid bright and unusual colours; the business community is still fairly conservative in nature. Resumés should be printed on good bond paper (at least 20 lb/75 g/m2). When using special shades or types of paper, use the same paper for your cover letters and other correspondence. Special resumé paper and envelopes can be found in most office supply stores. If you plan to send a number of resumés by fax, the paper quality is not so important. Always select a font style and size that is easy to read (see Tips on Formatting, above).

Photos

The use of photographs is not recommended. For most people, photos are not relevant to the positions they seek. However, there is a growing trend toward including photos on resumés displayed on the Internet. Most job-search experts, however, feel that photos can easily be used to discriminate against individuals. Therefore, unless your personal appearance is key to the position (such as jobs in the broadcast or movie industries), stay away from photographs.

Word Processing Software

While computers are sold with many different software programs, the only program that interacts well with those used by the majority of businesses is Microsoft Office. You should use only Microsoft Word to create your resumé. Often you will purchase your computer with Microsoft Works already installed. I recommend you not use this program or other software programs to create your resumé as it will likely not be compatible when you send it to a potential employer. If they can't open it, they will simply move on to the next resumé that they can open.

Resumé Writing Templates

Today, the computer makes many routine tasks easier and less tedious. Resumé writing is one of these tasks. There are many resumé software programs on the market. Although you may look into these programs as an alternative to typing everything from scratch, beware. Nothing takes the place of a carefully created, well-planned, and well-implemented original resumé.

When you rely on these canned programs, your resumé ends up looking like everyone else's. A case in point is the Microsoft Office resumé template. Because it is part of a commonly used suite of software programs, its format and style are easily recognized. Resumé templates make some tasks easier initially, but the trade-off is originality. Do you want your resumé to look like all the others? You will also find these templates very difficult to edit or manipulate. They are almost impossible to convert to a text-based resumé to upload onto a website.

Optimal Resumé

Optimal Resumé is an online program to which many colleges and universities are now subscribing. This program uses some of the template technology but brings it to a new level. The program will take you step by step though the data-entry portion while formatting it for you. However, the difference is that you then have many options that will customize and change the appearance with a click of the button. Once you are satisfied with the basic set-up, you pull it into your Microsoft Word program and further edit the appearance. Optimal Resumé will then save it in RTF (Rich Text Format). Optimal Resumé also assists by providing examples for typical positions, action verbs, and other tools that you will have the option of using along the way. Check with your Career Services department to see whether your school subscribes to this or other similar programs.

Final Check

As mentioned earlier, accuracy and correctness are critical. Proofread your resumé meticulously, not only for clearly presented information, but for grammar and spelling. Because the resumé is such an important document for your future career, it must not have any errors. Recruiters who see errors may conclude a couple of things about the writer. First, if there are spelling, grammar, or formatting errors, they may wonder how skilled this writer is. Second, if there are obvious spelling mistakes or other errors, they may assume that the writer is a careless person and conclude that this person may also be careless when performing the job.

Be a careful proofreader. Two techniques for proofing are reading backward and reading out loud. Read each word of your resumé, starting at the end of the last line and working your way to the left and to the top. This helps you uncover misspellings and typos. Reading your resumé out loud ensures readability and completeness. When proofing, examine the resumé for any mechanical errors. Word processing spellcheckers are a great way to catch the obvious mistakes, but they don't catch all of them.

Once you have finished proofing your resumé, show it to others whose opinions you value. Make any changes needed to improve the document at this point. Remember, resumé writing is very subjective. Everyone has an opinion, and there is no one right way to do it. Sometimes it is useful to seek out the opinions of others; however, if you receive too much conflicting advice, it is easy to become confused. Remember, this is *your* sales document. You must be satisfied with it. After all, you and only you will be the one to distribute it and talk about it during the interview.

Now, it is time to create (or update) your own resumé. Use the following as a final check before you get ready to print your copies.

RESUMÉ CHECKLIST

OVERALL APPEARANCE

_____ Are all the margins equal and does text appear balanced on the page?

_____ Is the content consistent in such elements as capitalization, verb tense, and punctuation?

_____ Are your key points either at the left margin or on the top half of the sheet?

_____ Does your name stand out, and are your address and phone number correct?

_____ Is your e-mail address professional and correct?

_____ Have you used bullets to make your statements easy to read?

CAREER OBJECTIVE

_____ If you have included this section, is the objective original?

_____ Is your objective specific to the position without limiting yourself too much?

_____ Did you put your statement in the third person and not use "my" or "I"?

PERSONAL SUMMARY

_____ If you have included this section, have you briefly described your accomplishments?

_____ Have you included specific personal skills?

_____ Have you included any experience with current electronic technology?

QUALIFICATIONS

_____ Have you listed your computer skills, including software you are experienced in using?

_____ Have you included any special training courses?

_____ Have you included any valid certificates or licenses such as CPR or WHMIS?

_____ Have you included all relevant skills that may not have been mentioned elsewhere?

_____ Have you included any professional memberships that are relevant?

_____ Have you provided the relevant skills learned from your education?

EDUCATION

_____ Have you included the correct title of your diploma/degree and the date it was granted?

_____ If a recent graduate, have you included your GPA?

WORK EXPERIENCE

_____ Have you included the names of the companies where you worked as well as the cities and provinces in which they are located?

_____ Have you included the terms of your positions, including the months and years?

_____ Have you remembered to include the titles of your positions?

_____ When you discussed your job responsibilities, were you descriptive and did you use action verbs whenever possible?

_____ Check through your job descriptions; do all the verb tenses agree with the time that you held the positions?

_____ Did you create scope and achievement statements?

_____ Did you omit managers' names, previous salary, and reasons for leaving?

_____ Have you included any co-op, field, or internship experience?

PERSONAL

_____ Have you provided meaningful and useful information?

_____ Have you included recent and relevant volunteer experience?

_____ Have you included relevant interests, associations, and activities?

RESUMÉ SAMPLES

Now that you have learned about resumé writing, let's look at some samples. Remember, how you organize and lay out your resumé on the page is just as subjective as what you choose to put into it. You must decide what looks best to you and what showcases your traits and skills most appropriately. Also, remember that it should be attractive and easy to read.

EXHIBIT 5.1   Sample chronological resumé

RYAN H. CHAN   **416-495-8892**
1221 Pleasent Hill Drive, Toronto, ON M59 2T9   rchan@linkup.com

OBJECTIVE

To secure the position of Programmer Analyst with IBC Enterprises

EDUCATION

May 2011

COMPUTER PROGRAMMER ANALYST - GRADUATE
Lambton College, Sarnia, ON

Honours:
GPA 3.90/4.00
Dean's Honour List

QUALIFICATIONS

- Demonstrated working ability with common hardware server and workstation platforms
- Practical experience with Networking Systems Linux, Windows Workstation/Server
- Programming languages used are Java, C, C++, Perl/Unix Shell script writing and Assembler
- Ability to analyze problem situations and generate creative solutions
- Apply structured approach to program design development testing and debugging
- French bilingual

WORK EXPERIENCE

2011–present

Operations Supervisor
SPEEDY PARCEL SERVICE CORPORATION, Toronto, ON

- Responsible for controlling production, efficiency, employee motivation, promotion and discipline
- Supervise 25 floor employees during second shift
- Demonstrated ability to apply workflow analysis
- Provide ongoing support of production applications systems including problem analysis, resolution, and reporting as necessary
- Design, construct, test, document, and implement new or existing applications
- Train new employees, hold communications meetings
- Evaluate employees in performance reviews

Sept.–Dec. 2010

Co-op
ABC AUTOMOTIVE PARTS, Toronto, ON

- Served as project leader for co-op consulting project
- Designed and implemented an inventory tracking system for automotive parts distributor, which improved efficiency by 20 percent
  Received an outstanding evaluation during my work term
- Gained experience with Java, C, C++

2009–2010

Destination Specialist
GROUND DELIVERY TRANSPORTATION, Toronto, ON
- Consulted with clients concerning systems operation
- Advised technical managers in operational techniques
- Conducted oral presentations for internal and external audiences

REFERENCES   Available upon request

EXHIBIT 5.2 Sample functional resumé

RYAN H. CHAN
1221 Pleasant Hill Drive
Toronto, ON   M5P 2T9
416-495-8892
rchan@linkup.com

OBJECTIVE

To secure the position of Programmer Analyst with IBC Enterprises

EDUCATION

COMPUTER PROGRAMMER ANALYST - GRADUATE May 2011
Lambton College, Sarnia, ON

Honours:

GPA 3.90/4.00
Dean's Honour List

SKILLS

Supervisory:

- Responsible for controlling production, efficiency, employee motivation, promotion, and discipline
- Supervisor of 25 floor employees during second shift
- Project leader for co-op consulting project

Technical:

- Demonstrated working ability with common hardware server and workstation platforms
- Practical experience with Networking Systems Linux, Windows Workstation/Server
- Programming languages used are Java, C, C++, Perl/Unix Shell script writing and Assembler
- Ability to analyze problem situations and generate creative solutions
- Apply structured approach to program design development testing and debugging
- Designed and implemented an inventory tracking system for automotive parts distributor, which improved efficiency by 20 percent
- Demonstrated ability to apply workflow analysis
- Provide ongoing support of production applications systems including problem analysis, resolution, and reporting as necessary
- Design, construct, test, document, and implement new or existing applications

Communication:

- Consulted with clients concerning systems operation
- Advised technical managers in operational techniques
- Trained new employees and held communications meetings
- Evaluated employees in job performance reviews
- Conducted oral presentations for internal and external audiences
- French bilingual

EMPLOYMENT

Operations Supervisor, July 2011–present
SPEEDY PARCEL SERVICE CORPORATION, Toronto, ON

Co-op, Sept.–Dec. 2010
ABC AUTOMOTIVE PARTS, Toronto, ON

Destination Specialist, 2009–2010
GROUND DELIVERY TRANSPORTATION, Toronto, ON

REFERENCES

Available upon request

EXHIBIT 5.3 | **Sample two-page resumé**

AISHA SMITH
11245 Anystreet, Sarnia, ON N2L 3H5 • 519-242-1047 • asmith@internet.net

OBJECTIVE

Hospitality Co-op position May–Aug. 2011

EDUCATION

HOSPITALITY & TOURISM MANAGEMENT   2009–present
Lambton College, Sarnia, ON
GPA 3.78/4.00
Candidate to graduate   August 2011

OSSD
St. Clair High School, Sarnia, ON

QUALIFICATIONS

- Smart Serve Certified
- Computer skills: Microsoft Office Word, Excel, PowerPoint, Internet, e-mail
- Cash-handling and balancing experience
- 5 years' customer service experience
- WHMIS trained
- Valid CPR certificate
- Basic French

EXPERIENCE

Front Desk Agent   2010–present
ANY HOTEL, Sarnia, ON

- Efficiently check guests in and out of 175 room full service hotel
- Provide excellent customer service advising guests on local attractions, restaurants and events
- Maintain hotel standards while following all procedures
- Accurately perform night audit
- Confirm reservations and determine appropriate nightly rate
- Work efficiently and accurately under pressure and with little or no supervision

Co-op Student/Server   May–Sept. 2010
ANY RESORT, Huntsville, ON

- Served food and beverage in the resort's fine-dining restaurant in a professional manner
- Familiar with all menu items and made recommendations for special diets
- Recommended appropriate wine with meals
- Advised guests on resort and local activities
- Received outstanding evaluation

Food and Beverage Server   2009–2010
ANY RESTAURANT, Sarnia, ON

- Served food and beverage in a busy family-style restaurant
- Provided friendly and excellent customer service
- Demonstrated ability to discuss all 185 menu items
- Assisted with basic food preparation
- Learned the value of team work
- Developed excellent time management and organizational skills

(Continued)

EXHIBIT 5.3   Sample two-page resumé (*Continued*)

AISHA SMITH

519-242-1047

VOLUNTEER

BIG SISTERS   Sarnia, ON
- Big Sister to 10-year-old girl for 1 year
- Active fundraiser for Big Sisters

CELEBRATION OF LIGHTS   Sarnia, ON
- Assist with set-up and take-down of annual event

INTERESTS

- Active in team sports including basketball and volleyball
- Member of the Lambton College Women's Volleyball Team
- Work out to maintain physical fitness
- Photography

PORTFOLIO

Available upon request

REFERENCES

Available upon request

EXHIBIT 5.4   **Other sample format**

CAROLYN STEVENSON

492 Middleton Lane
Calgary, AB TOM 3Y5

403-430-3758
stevenson@internet.ca

PROFESSIONAL SUMMARY

Areas of strength in accounting include:

- Cost Accounting, Federal Tax Accounting, Accounting Information Systems
- Microsoft Office - Word, Excel, MS Access, Accpac computerized accounting package
- Take pride in producing accurate calculation for data used by management for budgeting, forecasting, and sales projections. Capable of building excellent working relationships with professional staffs at all levels.
- Decision-making and leadership skills used to prioritize daily workload. Organize projects and written reports and records. Consistent follow-up on work environment to ensure deadlines are met on time and to specifications.

EMPLOYMENT

Tax Associate   2011–present
CLARK AND LEWIS ACCOUNTING SERVICE, Calgary, AB

- Perform tax compliance, analysis, and research for consolidated companies
- Provide tax consulting to partnerships, trustees, and non-profit organizations
- Awarded excellent rating for customer service

Accounting Assistant   2009–2011
ASPEN HILL RETIREMENT COMMUNITY, Windsor, ON

- Responsible for developing and presenting financial topics to residents
- Counselled individuals concerning personal finances
- Provided assistance to corporate controller in financial statement matters

EDUCATION

Bachelor of Commerce   2011
University of Windsor, Windsor, ON

Accounting Diploma   2008
Lambton College, Sarnia, ON

References available upon request

EXHIBIT 5.5 Text resumé for applying online

RYAN H. CHAN
1221 Pleasant Hill Drive
Toronto, ON M5P 2T9
416-495-8892
rchan@linkup.com
* * * * * * * * * * * * *

OBJECTIVE
To secure the position of Programmer Analyst with IBC Enterprises

EDUCATION

May 2011
COMPUTER PROGRAMMER ANALYST - GRADUATE
Lambton College, Sarnia, ON

* Honours
* GPA 3.90/4.00
* Dean's Honour List

QUALIFICATIONS

* Demonstrated working ability with common hardware server and workstation platforms
* Practical experience with Networking Systems Linux, Windows Workstation/Server
* Programming languages used are Java, C, C++, Perl/Unix Shell script writing and Assembler
* Ability to analyze problem situations and generate creative solutions
* Apply structured approach to program design development testing and debugging
* French bilingual

WORK EXPERIENCE

2011–present
SPEEDY PARCEL SERVICE CORPORATION, Toronto, ON

* Responsible for controlling production, efficiency, employee motivation, promotion, and discipline
* Supervise 25 floor employees during second shift
* Demonstrated ability to apply workflow analysis
* Provide ongoing support of production applications systems including problem analysis, resolution, and reporting as necessary
* Design, construct, test, document, and implement new or existing applications
* Train new employees, hold communications meetings

Sept.–Dec. 2010
ABC AUTOMOTIVE PARTS, Toronto, ON

* Served as project leader for co-op consulting project
* Designed and implemented an inventory tracking system for automotive parts distributor, which improved efficiency by 20 percent
* Received an outstanding evaluation during my work term
* Gained experience with Java, C, C++,

2009–2010
GROUND DELIVERY TRANSPORTATION, Toronto, ON

* Consulted with clients concerning systems operation
* Advised technical managers in operational techniques
* Conducted oral presentations for internal and external audiences

REFERENCES Available upon request

EXHIBIT 5.6   Sample scannable (key word) resumé

Cynthia Salazar

1347 Quincy Road, Toronto, ON M5P 2X3
416-555-8981
Email: salazarc@quicklink.com

Key Words: Bachelor's Degree in Business, 8 years analyst experience, experienced report writer, developed sales performance guidelines, experienced financial analyst, excellent presentation skills, team player, effective manager and leader, excellent sales performance, experience with contract sales force. Received sales award, increased sales by 15 percent. Hired, trained, and managed sales staff.

Work Experience

2011–Present Sales Analyst, Comco Products, Toronto, ON
- Formulate recommendations relative to sales performance data
- Perform analysis of both internal and external sales history
- Create reports for upper and mid-level management
- Deliver presentations on performance data and national trends
- Supervise task force group evaluating current sales concepts

2009–2010, Senior Sales Representative, Office Solutions, Edmonton, AB
- Supervised 12 junior sales associates in a four-state region
- Hired, trained, and managed new sales associates; analyzed performance of current general sales staff
- Managed own sales region of 23 locations with an average increase in sales of 15 percent

2008–2009, Sales Associate, Leland Homes, Toronto, ON
- Developed marketing plans and media placement for new home construction company
- Developed leads, contacted sales prospects, presented three different residential communities to clients
- Received Sales Associate of the Year Award for 20 percent increase in annual sales

Education

B.A. in Marketing, University of Toronto, Toronto, ON
Advanced Marketing Techniques Diploma, Sales Institute Inc.

References

REFERENCES

Although the resumé is critical to career success, another element to a successful job search must also be explored—finding and using references. Many questions such as these arise when thinking about selecting references:

- Do I really need to have references?
- Will they be checked?
- How many should I have?
- Whom should I select?
- What should they say about me?

Companies differ in their requirements for references, but most do want them and will check them. Employers want to ensure they are hiring the best people. They also want to know that they are hiring good people in general. When they begin checking references, they are fairly confident that you can handle the job and fit into the firm. They now want some reassurances from people who know you that their evaluation of you is correct. They want a final blessing, so to speak, before they continue with the hiring process.

So, when are references requested? Some companies want them upfront, others after the first interview or two. Others want them at the end of the interview process, but before they consider making a job offer. So, what should you do?

This information varies greatly depending on whom you speak to. Many experts suggest putting "References available upon request" at the bottom of your resumé. You would then take your references to an interview or wait for the potential employer to ask you for them. This is in fact the most common practice.

However, you need to remember that the purpose of submitting a resumé is to sell yourself by providing relevant information. Certainly references are part of this process, and providing them in advance indicates you are well-prepared in your application. Your reference list also gives additional insight to the employer and makes it easier to hire you.

Recruiters often expect that co-op students and recent graduates will provide references with the application. Because of the large volume of resumés they are looking through, often hurriedly, having references handy saves them a lot of time in the long run. There is also a growing trend among some employers to do reference checks prior to the interview. Even if your references are not needed at this time, submitting them in advance means at the very least that your application is complete.

The bottom line is you *do* need references, and they should be good ones. If recruiters ask you for references, they will be checked. Because it is not efficient to check references by mail, references are usually contacted by phone. Some employers are now checking references by e-mail or sending out fill-in-the-blank surveys through e-mail.

The dynamics of a telephone conversation are the best way to achieve the goals of both the recruiter and the person giving the reference. Let's take a look at some answers to frequently asked questions about references.

How Many References Should I Have?

Many people use three to five individuals. Some may be personal references and others may be professional ones. Keep in mind that when recruiters check references, they may just call the first and second names on the list. Others may work their way down the list until they reach someone. Some recruiters may contact each one listed.

Whom Should I Ask?

Currently, we refer to four categories of references: employment (past employers, co-workers), professional (business contacts, professional or community organization contacts), academic (professors, instructors, counsellors), and personal (people who know you personally). Whether you use three or four categories, you must decide how many you want in each. Remember to focus on work-related individuals. Never use members of your immediate family, and always select people who are articulate and fairly easy to contact. Most employers would rather speak to other employers, however, so this should be your first area of concentration.

Reference Formatting

It is usually recommended that you create a separate page to attach to your resumé or to take to an interview. This page should have a full header that matches the header on your resumé. The information should be presented in a professional manner that matches the rest of your resumé in both font style and paper. A sample reference list format is shown in Exhibit 5.7.

EXHIBIT 5.7   Reference list format

AISHA SMITH
11245 Anystreet, Sarnia, ON N2L 3H5 • 519-242-1047 • asmith@internet.net

REFERENCES

John Smith
General Manager
Any Hotel
123 Any St.
Sarnia ON N7T 1L5
(519) 542-2995
John.smith@anyhotel.com

Mary Garcia
Front Office Manager
Any Resort
123 Anylake Dr.
Huntsville ON M3V 5P7
(705) 339-1234
mgarcia@anyresort.ca

Sam Black
Professor
Lambton College
1457 London Rd.
Sarnia ON N7S 6K4
(519) 542-7751 Ext. 4444
sam.black@lambton.on.ca

What Should They Say About Me?

It depends. Professional references address your work ethic, the quality of your work, your personality on the job, and similar qualities. Academic references will comment about your class attendance, participation, punctuality, and your ability to get along with classmates. Personal references are asked about your character and personality in general.

Other Advice for Handling References

Get permission from your intended references before you give their names to prospective employers. Remember, you are asking these people to assist you in your job search. You want to be courteous about it, and you want them to be prepared. Tell your references about your job targets or your goals and make them aware of your most marketable traits. Alert them to any specific calls from employers they may receive. Inform them of the position that relates to the call and your qualifications for that position. Your references should speak as directly as possible to a particular opening and your ability to fill it. Ask your references if they prefer to be contacted at work or at home. It is also a good idea to find out the best time of the day or evening to contact them.

Determine which references will be most appropriate for you. Select people who are willing and eager to brag about you! At the same time, select people who converse easily and can handle potentially difficult questions. Also remember, people must be available to receive phone calls about you: Don't select someone who is always out of town or in meetings.

Be careful not to overuse people who have agreed to be your references. It may be useful to select two individuals as your key references and rotate their names to the top of your reference list. Also, call your references to let them know each time you give their names to potential employers. Tell them to expect the calls.

Choose your references based on their knowledge of you rather than on their prestige. Don't select someone who has an impressive title or position but very little knowledge about you.

Keep your references reasonably updated on the progress of your job search. Finally, remember to thank the people who serve as your references. The best call your reference can receive is one in which you tell them how happy you are in your new position!

Questions Your References Should Expect

What are some typical questions that references are asked? Different employers want to know different things so they may have unique questions. However, there are some common ones that you should make your references aware of.

1. What is your relationship to the candidate?
2. How long have you known the candidate?
3. When and why did he/she leave the job?
4. What was the candidate's attendance like at work?
5. What were his/her duties?
6. How was the candidate's cooperation with supervisors and co-workers?
7. What are the candidate's strengths?
8. What are the candidate's weaknesses?
9. How adaptable is the candidate to changes in the workplace?
10. Was he/she self-motivated?

11. How does this candidate handle stress?
12. What are the applicant's interpersonal and communication skills like?
13. Would you rehire the candidate if you had the opportunity?
14. Is there anything else you would like to add?

These sample questions are most appropriately asked of an employer. While recruiters may ask personal references some questions similar to these (such as "How long have you known the candidate?" and "What are the candidate's strengths?"), generally recruiters ask questions about a candidate's personality, honesty, character, and so on. When speaking to your academic references they will want to know about attendance, participation, quality of work, and consideration of classmates.

As you can see, selecting and using references goes well beyond casually asking a friend to be a reference. Exhibit 5.7 offered a format for your reference sheet that you may tailor to your own needs. Remember, have your reference sheet with you at all times while interviewing. This concludes the discussion of two very critical tools for any job search success: resumés and references. Both deserve your time and effort to develop. Both will serve you well in getting that job or changing to the career you have always dreamed about.

INTERNET RESUMÉ SITES

The following is a listing of some interesting locations on the Internet for further tips, examples, and advice. Please remember this: Sites on the Internet change constantly; therefore, some of the addresses below may be relocated or may have disappeared by the time you read this. Also, the listing of Internet sites in this book in no way indicates recommendations or endorsements by Pearson Canada or by the authors. These are listed for information only.

Workopolis:
www.workopolis.com

Quintessential Careers:
www.quintcareers.com

Monster:
www.monster.ca

Job Web:
www.jobweb.com

College Grad Job Hunter:
www.collegegrad.com

Job Hunters Bible:
www.jobhuntersbible.com

The Riley Guide:
www.rileyguide.com

MY Focus   ESPECIALLY FOR COLLEGE STUDENTS

1. How are resumés and references critical components of your self-promotion? Describe how they will assist you with your self-promotion.

2. Focusing on a possible personal summary for your resumé, what would you include as your top three traits?

3. For your reference list, how will your reference choices be able to market you? What will their knowledge of you be based on?

FINDING YOUR FOCUS

1. With your knowledge of reverse chronological and functional resumés, which one is the best for you and why?

2. Select either a current or past position and describe that position using duty, scope, and achievement statements.

3. How do you feel about the trend toward scanning resumés into scanning software? Is it a good idea? How can it work for and against you?

4. Develop your list of references, deciding how many and whom to include in each category: employment, professional, academic, and personal. Can you ever have too many references? What other assistance can references give you in your job search?

6

Career Correspondence and Applications

CHAPTER OBJECTIVES

After completing this chapter, you will be able to:

- Apply the proper writing techniques to create successful career correspondence.

- Produce a cover letter for your job-search needs.

- Produce other career correspondence as needed.

- Describe the role of the application in the job-search process.

- Complete a job application accurately and correctly.

Job-Search Necessities

Striving for success without hard work is like trying to harvest where you haven't planted.

—DAVID BLY

A successful job search cannot be conducted without a focus on the correspondence that's key to securing a position. This chapter discusses preparing cover letters and other necessary job-search correspondence, and completing a job application. Throughout the chapter, you'll find tips and techniques to help you prepare career correspondence and job applications thoroughly and accurately.

CAREER CORRESPONDENCE

When are job-search letters necessary? Quite often. First, there are cover letters that accompany your resumés. There are also networking letters, prospecting letters, follow-up letters after the interview, and finally (and happily) the acceptance letter. Let's begin with one of the most important pieces of correspondence, the cover letter.

The Cover Letter

A cover letter, or letter of application as it is sometimes called, is the letter that covers your resumé, literally. A cover letter introduces you to the potential employer. It makes a first impression and serves to set the tone for your resumé. A well-crafted cover letter contains useful information not found in your resumé and spotlights important items that are included in the resumé. So, it is a fairly important piece of writing.

Characteristics of a Good Cover Letter
A good cover letter does the following:

- Makes a good first impression.
- Is original and specific to each job application situation.

- Provides an answer to the question "Why should I hire you?"
- Is direct and to the point.
- Is one page or less in length.
- Matches your resumé, font style, and paper (if hard copy).

Writing the Cover Letter

Remember, a cover letter *must* be well written. Its purpose is to transmit and present your resumé to a recruiter. Because it establishes the very first impression of you, it must put your very best foot forward. Essentially, cover letters can be written in three or four basic paragraphs:

1. The introductory paragraph, in which you apply for the position, giving its title and how you learned about it.

2. The middle paragraph(s), which reference(s) your resumé and sell(s) you by mentioning your key attributes or traits. This section works well when it is divided into two separate paragraphs to highlight separate areas such as experience and skills and your education.

3. The closing paragraph, which asks for an interview and indicates the follow-up you will do.

These three parts of a successful cover letter are shown in Exhibit 6.1. A sample cover letter follows in Exhibit 6.2.

Sample Cover Letter In Response to an Advertisement

It is important to look at the advertisement and highlight the qualifications the company is looking for that match your own. Do not address the qualifications that you do not have. Sometimes you will find it useful to bold key points or bullet a list of qualifications in the letter. If the company uses a job number in the ad, it is very important to highlight this in your letter. When responding to an advertised position you must follow the directions. If it says no phone calls you must not follow up by phone or indicate that you will in your letter.

EXHIBIT 6.1 **Cover letter guidelines**

1412 Ontario Street
Toronto, ON
M5P 1L6

March 21, 2011

Mr. Jerry P. Smith, Vice President
Lakewood General Hospital
545 Weller Avenue
Toronto, ON M7N 2S3

Dear Mr. Smith:

Introductory Paragraph: In this paragraph, give the reason for the letter, name the specific position or type of employment for which you are applying, and mention how you learned about the opening.

Middle Paragraph: Indicate why you are interested in the position and company. Also state what you believe you can do for the company, and what contributions you can make to it. If you are a recent graduate, talk about your degree/diploma and how you feel that it and your other experiences qualify you for the position. If you are an experienced worker, point out your achievement or talents that make you a good candidate. You may be including some ideas similar to ones found in your resumé, but try not to use the very same wording. Finally, at the appropriate spot in this paragraph, refer the reader to your enclosed resumé, which further explains your qualifications and experience. This information is usually easier to separate into two paragraphs. These are the paragraphs that should make you appear the ideal candidate. Talk about the skills you have; don't mention what you don't have.

Closing Paragraph: Here you thank the reader and state your desire for an interview and your flexibility. You should include telephone numbers where you can be reached as well. As far as indicating what follow-up you will take, it is highly recommended that you be assertive and active in the closing of the letter and tell the reader that you will be following up with a telephone call to arrange an interview time. Some job-seekers end the letter in a more passive way with a basic statement that they look forward to hearing from the reader; however, the only place that statement gets them is sitting by the telephone waiting for it to ring. Take control: Tell the reader you will call and then do it, unless the advertisement or job posting indicates no phone calls.

Sincerely yours,

William H. Austin

William H. Austin

Enclosure

EXHIBIT 6.2 *Sample cover letter in response to an advertisement*

1225 Hampton Avenue
Edmonton, AB
T8L 2N5

March 12, 2011

Mr. Derik C. Stephenson
Director of Human Resources
Peterson Industries
1345 West Edmonton Mall Road
Edmonton, AB T9C 3S9

Dear Mr. Stephenson:

Please consider my application for the position of **Administrative Assistant** which was
advertised on March 10th with Career Services at Western College. The position is an
excellent match with my education, experience, and career interests.

With a major in Office Administration at Western College, I have training on Microsoft
Office 2007, as well as training and experience with a variety of software programs and
applications. My program provided both extensive theory and practical applications for
Word, Excel, Access, Outlook, and Power Point. My training has also included Simply
Accounting, Desktop Publishing, and Web Page design, as well as file management, proper
letter, e-mail, and memo etiquette, and general office management, as you have requested
in your advertisement.

My hands-on experience assisting students, staff, faculty, and external customers as an
office assistant at Western College has enhanced my interpersonal communications skills.
In addition, I have been employed as a student worker with a large credit union, where
I gained valuable knowledge of financial systems software. As you will see in my enclosed
resumé, my education, experience, and career goals match your requirements well. I am
extremely interested in the Administration Assistant position and in working for
Peterson Industries.

Please consider my request for an interview to discuss my qualifications further. I will
contact you in the near future to see if a meeting can be arranged. If you would like to
reach me before then, please call me at 403-665-7828. Thank you for your consideration.
I look forward to meeting and talking with you.

Sincerely,

Charlene Parson

Charlene Parson

Enclosure

Prospecting Cover Letter

Sending prospecting letters is one method to get your name and qualifications in front of a wide variety of people. Generally, these letters are used when there is no clear or advertised opening, yet you have an interest in the company and want to send a letter to check out your "prospects." While your job search should not be composed only of prospecting letters, they can enhance your chances of getting hired. While this is another type of cover letter, you must guess the type of qualifications they are looking for. It is also critical that you conduct a follow-up with this type of letter.

EXHIBIT 6.3   **Sample prospecting cover letter**

850 Baldwin Avenue
Ridgetown, ON
N0P 2C0

February 12, 2011

Mr. Tony Lawrence
Director of College Recruiting
Northern Apple Association
1232 University Avenue
Toronto, ON M5L 6P9

Dear Mr. Lawrence:

In a recent issue of *The Globe and Mail* I read about your company. I would like to inquire into employment opportunities in your **sales trainee** program. My goal is to work in retail sales and management, and I would like to relocate to Toronto after graduation.

As an upcoming graduate from a three-year Business Marketing program, I am eager to apply my skills with a growing company such as yours. My education has provided a solid foundation in both the theory and practical aspects of the retail industry.

Sales opportunities have always interested me and I have held a variety of sales and marketing positions in high school and college, as you will see in my enclosed resumé. My co-op with Jones & Company, a large department store, convinced me that sales and marketing are the fields for me. As I read about your company, it seemed to me that it provides the kind of professional retail environment that I seek. My previous employers will tell you I have demonstrated a strong work ethic, creativity, and excellent customer service.

Thank you for reviewing my resumé. I look forward to meeting with you in person to discuss my qualifications. I will contact you in the near future to discuss a convenient time. I can be reached at (519) 666-9999.

Sincerely,

Craig Bandeau

Craig Bandeau

Enclosure

Networking Letter

Networking letters are an important part of your job search. This correspondence can increase your number of contacts and find people to help you in your job search. Exhibit 6.4 demonstrates a typical networking letter.

EXHIBIT 6.4   **Sample networking letter**

2929 Appleton Court
Woodstock, ON
N6P 3L5

April 20, 2011

Ms. Marlene Walker, Director
Jones, Walker, and Smith
1400 Commerce Dr., Suite 201
London, ON N7P 5B6

Dear Ms. Walker:

Dr. Myron Olsen, professor of law at the University of Western Ontario and a personal friend of my parents, suggested that I contact you. He thought that you, as a corporate lawyer, might be in an excellent position to assist me with a decision relating to my career.

As a law student, I am exploring different paths of employment. Corporate law, media law, and tax and financial law all sound interesting to me at this point, but I want to begin my job search next term with a clearer understanding of these options. I would like to hear your opinion of these areas and get a glimpse of a corporate law office in action.

I will be calling you in the near future to see if we can arrange a brief meeting at your convenience. Thank you for considering my request. I can be reached at (519) 333-1111.

Sincerely,

Janet R. Counsel

Janet R. Counsel

Thank-You Letter

All successful job candidates have one thing in common: spending time following up and following through. Developing skills lists, updating resumés, even having a good cover letter won't help if you don't follow up on contacts and interviews. Employers expect it. In fact, a recruiter once commented that he did not bother to call anyone who did not contact him after the interview. Recruiters want to know that you want them. They expect you to assert yourself and go after the position by being aggressive but not obnoxious. One way to accomplish this is to send thank-you letters after each interview. A typical thank-you letter is shown below. Chapter 9 discusses thank-you letters further.

EXHIBIT 6.5 | **Sample thank-you letter**

1225 Hampton Avenue
Edmonton, AB
T8L 2N5

April 20, 2011

Mr. Derik C. Stephenson
Director of Human Resources
Peterson Industries
1345 West Edmonton Mall Road
Edmonton, AB T9C 3S9

Dear Mr. Stephenson:

Thank you for the opportunity to interview with you yesterday for the position of Systems Analyst. I really enjoyed meeting you and learning more about your consulting operations and financial records systems.

As I stated in the interview, the requirements for your position and my qualifications are a match. I have training and experience with the systems you use, plus I have excellent communications skills and can deal effectively with individuals on a variety of levels. I'm certain that I would fit into your team and would ultimately make a significant contribution to your firm.

Again I would like to stress my strong interest in your company.
Thank you for your continued consideration.

Sincerely,

Charlene Parson

Charlene Parson

Acceptance Letter

The most joyful letter you may ever write is the acceptance letter. What is it and when is it used? An acceptance letter is sent to someone who made you a job offer that you plan to accept. Many offers are made verbally, and it is always a good idea to have the particulars of the offer in writing. Therefore, if the potential employer does not put the offer in writing (either initially or as a follow-up to the verbal offer), it is a good idea for you to draft an acceptance letter. There also may be times when the potential employer does put the offer in writing, and you may still wish to respond with your own acceptance letter. A sample acceptance letter is shown below.

EXHIBIT 6.6   **Sample acceptance letter**

---

34 Millbank Drive
London, ON
N2L 7X7

July 29, 2011

Ms. Jennifer Kutkowski
Senior Employment Specialist
Apex Communication Company
London, ON N5P 1X7

Dear Ms. Kutkowski:

Please consider this letter my acceptance of your July 28th offer of the position of network administrator for Apex Communication. I am delighted that I will soon be joining your fine firm. I look forward to making a contribution to your organization, and I appreciate the opportunity you have given me.

As we discussed on the 28th, I will report to work at 8:00 a.m. on Monday, August 24th, and will have completed the required physical examination by that time. My starting salary will be $40,000 annually, and I will receive a performance review after six months of service. I will be reporting to Mr. Harold White as one of his junior network administrators.

I look forward to working with Mr. White and joining the team at Apex Communication. I will report to your office on August 24th to fill in the required personnel forms. Thank you again.

Sincerely,

James Herrman

James Herrman

Final Tips on Letter Writing

Having examined the various types of job-search correspondence, there are a few final tips to keep in mind when creating any type of business correspondence. When typing the name of the recipient, use the proper courtesy title. The abbreviation "Mr." poses no problem because it is used for both married and unmarried men. When addressing females, it is safest to use "Ms." in all cases, unless the person has specified "Mrs." or "Miss."

In addition to the courtesy title, proper spelling is also very important. If you are uncertain as to the spelling of a person's name, call the company and ask for the correct spelling. Remember, even simple names like Smith or Johnson can be spelled different ways. Also concerning names, don't assume certain names are either masculine or feminine. Frances could be a man, and Taylor could be a woman. Call to make sure. Also, if the addressee has a title, use it. Most people like to see their names and titles in print, and they definitely want to see them spelled correctly!

Do you know why a letter has the writer's name typed at the end? This is included in case the recipient cannot read your signature. When sending business correspondence, sign the letter above your typed name. Also, if you are enclosing your resumé, be sure to type the word "Enclosure" underneath the signature block. This tells the reader that there is something else in the envelope or attached to the e-mail. Also, as you did with the resumé, punctuate correctly and check carefully for misspellings and typographical errors.

Finally, it is a good idea to keep copies of all your job-search correspondence. When you are in the middle of a busy job-search campaign, it is helpful to review items you sent. Keep photocopies or save them on your computer.

A Few Words on E-mail

With technology having such a big impact on business correspondence today, it is necessary to say a few words about e-mail as it pertains to business correspondence. Both e-mail and instant messaging are two popular ways for individuals to communicate practically instantaneously in both personal and professional settings. E-mail has become the accepted norm for all purposes and types of professional communications. So the question becomes "Is e-mail appropriate for career correspondence?" The first rule of thumb is to apply as requested in the job posting. In the last couple of years the majority of employers want to receive the applications either by e-mail or online. As mentioned previously, there are varied viewpoints. Some people feel e-mail is most appropriate for sending cover letters and resumés to recruiters because it is an efficient and contemporary technique. Others believe it is too casual a medium for this type of correspondence and is easily ignored or spammed.

You will have to decide on the most appropriate way to let potential hiring authorities know who you are and why they should pay attention to your correspondence. In some instances, the application process is done online, so there is no choice. In others, the decision is yours. The **Companion Website** provides links to Internet sites that discuss writing useful, effective cover letters.

INTERNET SITES

Use the Internet sites listed on page 80 of Chapter 5, Resumés and References, for additional information.

JOB APPLICATIONS

In addition to letters, another written component of the job-search process is the job application. Will it be necessary to complete an application? In almost all cases, the answer is yes. Most companies still use job applications and must have completed applications on file before offers are extended. Because job applications are still a common requirement for employment, be prepared to fill them out at any point in the job-search process.

When you apply for a position, whether in person, online, or through the mail, you may receive a job application. The application may be mailed to you, or you may be asked to complete it online or when you arrive for your first interview. No matter when you are asked to complete the application, keep the techniques discussed below in mind.

Again we need to discuss the Internet, as many application forms are now online. Ensure you follow the same strategies for completing online applications as you would for pencil-and-paper forms. It is critical that you complete all sections properly. Many companies set up the application to weed out improperly answered applications; in other words, they never get to the recruiter.

Getting Ready

To help you in completing an application form, have a copy of your resumé with you, or even a prepared master application to refer to. It is not acceptable to leave an application blank and write instructions to see your attached resumé, or to submit your own prepared application. However, having a copy of your resumé or a master application to refer to can save you time and help ensure accuracy as you fill out the real one. Online applications often begin with creating a profile that you will complete on the website. Then every time you come back to that particular website to apply for another position, that part of the application is already done for you. It is important to remember to check and update your profile every time you apply to a new position. If you don't, you run the risk that the website will simply thank you for applying for the position and use the previous profile, resume, and cover letter on file—even if your previous application was six months before.

Before completing the application, read it thoroughly, no matter how many you have submitted previously. Each company's application may be just a bit different, so pay attention. Fill out the application completely and honestly. Do not omit or misrepresent anything. The falsification of application information can be grounds for immediate dismissal. Most applications have a space for your signature and the date at the end. Don't forget to sign it. Signing an application indicates that you affirm the completeness and accuracy of the document.

Print clearly and do not skip lines or sections of the application. If a line or section doesn't apply to you, simply write N/A for "not applicable" in the appropriate spaces or place a small line in that section or box. It is not necessary (and would be difficult at best) to try to type your responses on an application.

Some recruiters say that they notice how careful job candidates are (or aren't) when filling out applications. Be neat. Also, recruiters say they are interested in viewing a candidate's handwriting, so be sure your writing is legible! Here are five tips to keep in mind when preparing to fill out a job application.

Tips for Completing a Job Application

1. *Always use black ink.* Although pencil can be erased, it smudges easily and is harder to read. Do not use markers or gel pens.

2. *Check directions carefully.* Does the application ask you to print or write? What other specific directions does it give you? Remember to read the entire application before writing.

3. *Use correct spelling.* Be very careful; make sure you can spell all of the terms and words connected to your work. Don't misspell names of companies. Don't guess at any spellings; be sure before you begin.

4. *Be careful how you handle sections on salary.* The best place to talk about salary is in an interview, not in an application. Therefore, it may be best to write "Open" or "Negotiable" if requested to indicate salary expectations. Any information on past salary history should be accurate.

5. *Practice makes perfect.* Practise by filling out the application on pages 93–94 (Exhibit 6.7). Have it available when applying for jobs so you can ensure accuracy, correctness, and neatness when you fill in the actual application.

Illegal Questions

You may be asked illegal questions on an application form. You will have to decide for yourself what you will answer, but you need to know what it is illegal to ask you.

On application forms it is not acceptable to include questions about the following: race, ancestry, place of origin, colour, ethnic origin, citizenship, creed, sex, sexual orientation, age, record of offences, marital status, same-sex partnership status, family status, or handicap. Questions pertaining to employment-related medical examinations or medical inquiries that are part of the screening process are also not allowed.

However, it is legal to ask if the candidate is legally eligible to work in Canada, or if the candidate has the skills needed to perform the job.

For further information, consult the website of the Ontario Human Rights Commission at www.ohrc.on.ca/english/index.shtml. While this information is specifically for Ontario, the other provinces have similar laws.

EXHIBIT 6.7   **Sample employment application form**

ACORN CELLULAR

Personal Information   Date_____

Name Last		First	Middle
Present Address	Street		City
Province		Postal Code	
Permanent Address	Street		City
Province		Postal Code	
Phone Number		**Referred By**	

Employment Desired

Position	Date You Can Start	Salary Desired
Are You Presently Employed?	If So, May We Contact of Your Present Employer?	

Education

Name & Location of School	Years Attended	Date Graduated	Major/Program
Post-secondary			
Trade, Business, or Correspondence			
High School			

General

Subjects of special study or research work
What foreign languages do you speak fluently?   Read?   Write?
Are you legally eligible to accept employment in Canada?   ❑ Yes   ❑ No

Work-Related Skills

Describe any relevant skills, certificates, licenses, or training.

Continued

EXHIBIT 6.7   **Sample employment application form**   *(Continued)*

Former Employers (List below your last four employers, starting with most recent one first)

Date/Month/Year	Employer Name and Address	Salary	Position	Reason for Leaving
From To				
Responsibilities				
From To				
Responsibilities				
From To				
Responsibilities				
From To				
Responsibilities				

References (Give below the names of three persons not related to you whom you have known at least one year)

Name	Address	Business	Years Known

I authorize investigation of all statements contained in this application. I understand that misrepresentation or omission of facts called for is cause for dismissal.

Signature	Date

Whenever you fill out a job application, keep these three points in mind:

■ Supply complete information.
■ Be honest.
■ Write legibly.

MY Focus — ESPECIALLY FOR COLLEGE STUDENTS

Your cover letter is a wonderful opportunity for self-promotion; that's the goal of this piece of career correspondence. Try this before you begin to craft your letter:

1. Find an advertisement for an opening in which you have interest. List three technical/business/career skills you have that qualify you for that position.

2. List three personal or nontechnical skills you could use to promote yourself for this position.

3. Examine the job description and match your skills to the traits desired.

4. Structure your letter in such a way that you are proving, point by point, that you have the requisite skills or experience for this job.

5. Finish by writing a "marketing" sentence that lets the company know that you are the candidate that they should interview.

Now, combine all of these steps for a tailor-made cover letter. Repeat the process for each position for which you wish to apply.

FINDING YOUR FOCUS

1. What are the functions of each of the paragraphs of the cover letter?

2. How should cover letters used in your job search be different from each other? Why?

3. What is the difference between a prospecting cover letter and a networking letter, and how might you employ each in your job search?

4. What are the three key points to keep in mind when filling out a job application?

5. Complete the sample application form. Have a friend check it for errors or incomplete information.

Professional Portfolios

After completing this chapter, you will be able to:

- Illustrate the importance of the professional portfolio in today's job search.

- Outline the different types of portfolios and determine how to select appropriate samples.

- Plan, format, and assemble a professional portfolio.

- Define the electronic portfolio.

- Effectively use a portfolio in career interviews.

A Way to Prove Yourself

Every job is a self-portrait of the person who does it. Autograph your work with excellence.

—UNKNOWN

As a job candidate today, you need all the ammunition you can get to succeed in your job search. There is more competition for available jobs, employers tend to be more skeptical of what candidates say they can do, and recruiters want to be sure they are making the best choices possible when they invite individuals to join their firms. An important tool to have in your job search is the professional portfolio. This tool contains samples of your finest work, whether taken from academic experiences and assignments or from previous work experiences and projects.

The use of portfolios by savvy job candidates is increasing. They realize that employers are very interested in seeing first-hand how and how well candidates can demonstrate their skills and perform their work. Tangible examples of these skills and capabilities are useful weapons.

The portfolio is an extremely effective tool to help achieve the important goal of proving yourself. It focuses the employer (and you) on your relevant skills and experiences. It moves you well past merely talking about yourself on paper as you did in your resume. It is a powerful and dynamic interview aid. Portfolios are useful to the most confident of candidates as well as to individuals who are a bit uncomfortable with selling themselves in an interview situation. Once you have a professional portfolio prepared, you will have numerous opportunities to use it in the interview process, and you will find that this tool helps you to be a confident, impressive candidate.

This chapter on professional portfolios addresses portfolio skills assessment, the selection of and types of samples, sample items, and portfolio planning, formatting, and compiling. Finally, there are discussions on electronic portfolios and using the portfolio you created.

PORTFOLIO SKILLS ASSESSMENT

The skills that employers seek have been discussed in previous chapters. Now, let's focus on critical skills and personal abilities that employers seek and are eager to see you demonstrate or document.

Skills and Personal Abilities to Demonstrate in Your Portfolio

1. Problem-solving skills. Can you assess circumstances and develop solutions? Can you develop plans to solve various problems?

2. Communication skills. Are you able to organize your thoughts clearly and communicate those thoughts effectively? Are you a good speaker and a good writer? Are you able to persuade others?

3. Resource allocation skills. Can you manage your time effectively? Can you manage resources well?

4. Technical skills. How proficient are you in the knowledge and skills in your course of study or technical field? How knowledgeable and skilled are you in the technology for your area, including any computer programs?

5. Teamwork skills. Do you work well with others? Do you shoulder your share of responsibilities in team settings? Do you demonstrate a commitment to the team or group?

6. Leadership skills. Can you inspire others and help them to bring out the best they have? Can you help those who work for you to meet stated goals and objectives?

7. Conflict management skills. How do you help others who are in conflict? Do you look for the best resolution for all parties involved? Can you deal with stressful situations and disagreeable people?

8. Self-confidence. How confident are you in your personal resources and abilities? How can you demonstrate your confidence?

9. Initiative. Are you able to see what needs to be done without having someone tell you? Do you initiate action? Do you follow up on commitments?

10. Quality. Are you committed to doing high-quality work? Do you work up to the standards given to you and do you set your own high standards?

11. Drive. Are you enthusiastic and motivated in your work and personal life? Do you have reserves of energy and enthusiasm that you can draw upon?

12. Imagination. Are you creative? Can you develop new and different ideas and solutions to problems? Can you see issues from different angles?

13. Flexibility. How adaptable are you to change? Are you open to and do you welcome new situations and ideas? Can you roll with things when necessary?

14. Goal achievement. Are you a realistic goal setter, and do you know how to work toward and meet those goals? Can you stay dedicated to goals and objectives when your abilities are challenged?

Once you have worked your way through this list of questions, you are ready to determine which portfolio materials will best reflect these skills and personal competencies. A Portfolio Skills and Personal Abilities worksheet is included on the **Companion Website** to help you generate answers to the above questions.

In addition to assessing your skills and personal abilities, it is important for you to examine your school, work, and life experiences to identify any accomplishments that are relevant to your job search and important in developing your professional portfolio. Ask yourself: What are the accomplishments of which I am most proud? These accomplishments usually come from activities that brought you the most satisfaction—for example, at school, at work, at home, in sports, in music or art, while volunteering, and so forth. Summarize three to five of your strongest accomplishments. This list is an excellent resource for the later steps of portfolio sample selection and development.

SELECTION OF AND TYPES OF SAMPLES

Depending on your specific skills and competencies, any of several types of sample materials can be included in the portfolio. As part of this portfolio preparation process, continue to develop lists of your prominent skills and abilities, both technical and nontechnical, and consider a variety of documents and examples that demonstrate these specific skills. For example, if your goal is to demonstrate computer programming skills, select a particularly challenging program you wrote or debugged. The following are suggested sample materials.

Resumé/Statement of Career Goals

The resumé is a good beginning for a professional portfolio. Also, listing your career goals helps potential employers understand what you are looking for and determine how well your plans match what they need in an employee. Goals are also a good way to demonstrate to employers that you are focused on future achievement.

Work Samples

Samples of your work might include materials from school projects, classes, or labs; on-the-job accomplishments that demonstrate your work skills, including professional presentations; work projects such as proposals, manuals, or other written documents; employer evaluations or summaries of performance reviews; and correspondence and multimedia presentations.

Certifications, Diplomas, Degrees, and Awards

This category covers copies of special achievements and recognitions of your work, technical certifications, diplomas from training programs, and newspaper or newsletter articles relating to your awards or achievements.

Community Service/ Volunteer Work

Documents, letters of recognition, photos, brochures, and similar items serve to show your contribution to community service projects. Include any written materials you developed as a part of your service or volunteer efforts.

Academic Record/ Transcript

Include a copy of your program of study or unofficial transcript that shows the courses completed for your degree and grades achieved. Official course outlines could also be included, especially for technical courses relevant to your goal.

Letters of Recommendation/ Commendation

These are letters from professors, supervisors, managers, or colleagues who have worked with you and can testify to your accomplishments; and commendation letters or memos received in recognition of special performance or contributions. Included in this category may be customer letters of recognition as well.

Electronic Materials

These materials include CDs, disks, videos, websites, or other electronic samples that show outstanding and unique achievements, including graphics, multimedia, and sound files.

Obviously if you are not a new graduate, you should supply a greater number of work samples and achievements and possibly omit your academic record, depending on how long it has been since you were in school. If you are a new graduate, include your academic record and any work achievements you have had while in school or over the summer. And don't forget that as a student you can generate impressive letters of recommendation as well!

PLANNING THE PORTFOLIO

The first step is to clarify your portfolio's message. Why are you putting it together? What does it say about you? What exactly are you stating or proving with the samples you have selected? What impression do you want this tool to make? By writing out your portfolio's message, you are organizing and selecting the materials to use. All samples in the portfolio should in some way support your written goal. This message does not go into your portfolio; it is for your own use and will help you put together the most focused portfolio possible.

Sample Message

My portfolio demonstrates that I can develop and implement networked computer systems that contribute to workplace efficiency. It proves that I am a good business communicator, effective problem solver, and valuable team member.

A message like this can not only help clarify your portfolio's goal, it can also be a handy statement to use when describing yourself to the employer! In addition to developing your portfolio's message, you should make a solid statement of goals for the employer to see. Listing career goals in your portfolio can help potential employers understand you, understand what you want in a career, and see how you would make a good employee. Career goals also demonstrate that you are a career- and goal-oriented person who wants to continue to achieve for yourself and for your employer. The following are suggested guidelines for developing three to five goals for your portfolio:

- Focus on the professional skills, knowledge, and achievements you want to pursue over the next two to five years.
- Ask yourself where you see yourself professionally four to five years from now. What do you want your accomplishments to be?
- Make your goals more specific than career objectives, focusing on specific accomplishments whenever possible. These goals should be measurable so you can tell when you have accomplished them.

Sample Goals Statement

- To hold a team or leadership role in IT projects.
- To develop project management skills by working with project managers and project personnel and by successfully using project management software tools.
- To earn outstanding performance reviews and receive promotions.
- To mentor new employees or trainees in the IT department.

Sometimes it is easier for an experienced individual to write goal statements because she has been working in the industry or field and able to draw from previous goals and performances. However, this should not deter new graduates. As a new college graduate, having a portfolio goals statement says to the potential employer that you are a person with vision and self-knowledge, the type of person he wants to employ.

Primary Skill Areas

As you plan your portfolio, you will see that the body, which includes your samples, must be organized in a logical pattern. This is the meat of your portfolio, so you must select your samples with great care and purpose. To do this, choose three to five primary skill areas that you want to demonstrate. These could include the following:

- Technical skills: computer programming, electronics engineering, project management, accounting, medical systems.
- Transferable skills: data gathering, analysis, planning, research, problem solving, conflict management.
- Functional skills: persuasion or sales, using technology, understanding business operations.
- Personal skills: writing, speaking, collaborating, leading, negotiating.

Once you have chosen the skill areas to emphasize, organize your samples into the appropriate categories. Use a separate category called "Other" for those materials, including electronic ones, that don't readily fit into any other category.

The next step in planning your portfolio is organizing your materials. Your message statement can help you organize the sections of your portfolio so they best represent you. Just as no one resumé format fits every candidate, no one portfolio format works for everyone either. Let your own talents, strengths, and message be your guide.

Organizational Structure

Below is one organizational structure that may be useful in putting together your portfolio, but consider your own individual characteristics before adopting a format.

1. Resumé and/or Statement of Goals
2. Thematic or Skills Areas
3. Academic Record
4. Certifications, Diplomas, Degrees, Awards
5. Community Service
6. Letters of Recommendation/Other Correspondence
7. Other (electronic)

Remember, your portfolio may contain all or only some of these categories, depending on your personal needs. Avoid the tendency to put too much into your portfolio as this will get you nowhere. Busy recruiters don't have the time to wade through endless examples and documents. Choose your content carefully to support your portfolio's message.

Organizational Techniques

Your portfolio should have particular elements that make its organization clear to the reader. Consider the following and decide which one or ones will work best for you.

Table of Contents

This should come at the very beginning of the portfolio. It is useful because it gives the reader an overview of what is inside. List the categories and the samples by name and indicate the pages where they are located.

Annotated Table of Contents

Although this is similar to a regular table of contents, it includes a bit more. Underneath each entry in the table of contents, include a brief description of what the sample is and what skills or abilities it demonstrates.

Cover Pages

These are created to introduce each portfolio section. They might be tabbed sheets that unify the separate elements of the portfolio while allowing the reader to see all of the units or categories at once. This particular type of formatting is discussed later in the chapter.

Labelling Samples

These are short overviews written for each sample. (These overviews can also appear in an annotated table of contents.) At the top of each sample, include the following information:

- What the sample is.
- What it is for, why it was done.
- When it was done.
- Who else was involved.
- What skills it demonstrates.

Statement of Originality

Last, you may want to include a statement of originality or confidentiality in your portfolio. This helps to protect the contents from being duplicated and protects any proprietary materials that may be included. This statement may say that the portfolio is your original work and cannot be copied without permission. It may also state that some of the materials are private and proprietary and should not be copied without permission.

FORMATTING THE PORTFOLIO

Now that you have organized your portfolio, turn your attention to its format. Because we live in a very visual society, visual cues are important for getting attention. Therefore, you must pay particular attention to good visual design.

Good visual design achieves the following: gains the reader's attention, clarifies and supports the document's organization, helps the reader understand the message, adds credibility, and demonstrates professionalism. These achievements make it clear why it is so crucial to spend time on good visual design. The following tips will assist you with your visual design plan.

Visual Perception Tips

- When people read in our culture, their eyes move from upper left to lower right on a page.
- People tend to start reading where the strongest visual element exists on a page.
- People notice illustrations before they notice text.
- People perceive larger items as more important than smaller ones. The same is true for larger headings as opposed to smaller ones.
- People pay attention to colour more than any other visual feature.

To discuss visual elements and your portfolio, let's examine typography, titles and headings, graphics or images, placement of elements, colour, and white space.

Typography

Your choice of fonts creates a look and feel for your portfolio. The two main font categories are serif and sans serif. Decorative fonts also exist but typically they are not suitable for resumé or portfolio use. Serif letters are accented with ornamental lines at the end. Examples of this font type are Times, Century Schoolbook, and

Garamond. Serif fonts are commonly believed to be easier to read in large blocks of type. Sans serif letters are straight and lack ornamentation. Examples of this font type are Arial, Helvetica, and Optima. Sans serif fonts are often used for headings and as display type. Decorative fonts are more elaborate versions of either serif or sans serif fonts. Examples are Stencil or Onyx fonts.

Which font is best for your portfolio? As with many other aspects of personal portfolio development, you are best qualified to determine which fonts you want to use. However, there are guidelines for the good use of typography.

Typgraphly Guidelines

- Body text is commonly a serif font in 10, 11, or 12 point size.
- Titles and headings are usually sans serif in 16 to 18 point size.
- Decorative fonts should be used sparingly, if at all. They tend to be difficult to read.
- Two fonts are the maximum for one page—one for text and one for headings.

In addition to these guidelines, here are a few additional suggestions for font usage and layout:

- Use all capital letters sparingly, and don't overuse bold and italics.
- Don't underline text; use bold or italics when necessary.
- Single-space body text; double-space before and after headings.
- Use one-inch margins all around.
- Don't cram a lot of text onto one page.

Title, Headings, and Captions

These components can be formatted to attract the eye. For your portfolio, use them to demonstrate a skill, show an action, or clarify something. Remember to use consistent formatting for each example of an element. For example, all titles should be treated consistently, all captions should be treated consistently, and so forth.

Graphic Images

Graphic images may include photos, illustrations, maps, charts, and other visual aids.

Use graphic images to break up text and provide variety on the page. Make sure your graphics are easy to understand and relay an important message. Always use high-quality images. Never frustrate your reader with a fuzzy or poorly rendered image. You might consider using borders around your graphic images to give them a formal, finished look.

Placement of Elements

A fact of visual placement is that the reader's attention can be directed by placing objects or visual cues in a sequence such as left to right or top to bottom. With that in mind, place the most important information near the top of the page. This was true for your resumé, and it is true for your portfolio.

When the eye is at rest, it tends to move to the bottom left section of a page, sometimes referred to as the visual hotspot. Place important messages in the visual hotspots for extra attention. Finally, a border or frame around a title or cover page gives it a more professional look and draws the eye inward on the page.

Colour

Colour is powerful and creates immediate impressions. Use colour to accentuate or differentiate elements. Examples include colour-coding sections of the portfolio or highlighting important elements or information in the same colour. However you decide to use colour, use it consistently to keep a professional look. Keep your colours easy on the eye, not garish or too bright. Don't overdo colour in your portfolio. This tends to make it look unprofessional and somewhat juvenile.

White Space

This is the blank area around text and graphics. The use of white space affects readability. Too little of it causes the page to look cramped and uninviting. Too much of it makes the page look unimportant or confusing, causing problems with where to focus first. If your pages look too crowded or incomplete and confusing, adjust the white space accordingly. Remember, a common problem with layout is placing too much information on a page.

A discussion of portfolio development is not complete without advice on presenting portfolio samples. The following tips should be kept in mind when you are preparing your samples for presentation.

Advice for Presenting Samples

Paper
Use the same paper throughout. Use high-quality, heavy bond paper, not thin photocopy or printer paper. You may want to use coloured paper in subtle shades to colour-code sections or accentuate important items.

Cropping
If you want to show just part of a sample, cut a window out of a blank sheet of paper and lay the new frame over your sample to crop what you don't want. Then, photocopy the new page for a finished look.

Videos, CDs, Computer Disks, DVDs
If you have to include a videotape, use VHS half-inch format, not 8mm or other formats. Make sure your tape is labelled. If supplying a computer disk, CD, or DVD, make sure the label identifies what is on the disk and clearly explains how to use or open it.

Clip Art
Use clip art only if it will enhance your message and look professional. Avoid cartoons or childish artwork. Stay away from overused, basic clip art that lacks imagination. All graphics in your portfolio must have a purpose and look professional.

ASSEMBLING THE PORTFOLIO

Now that all your hard work of planning and formatting is done, it's time to pull it all together. Find a clean, flat space to organize and assemble your items. Have all necessary supplies and materials nearby so you can put things together smoothly and efficiently.

Supplies

Supplies include a three-ring binder or zippered portfolio. These can be cloth, vinyl, or leather but not paper. A binder or portfolio two or three inches wide should be suitable, depending on the number of samples included. Try not to fit too many samples into a binder that's too small (one inch), and try not to use too large a binder (three inches) for too few samples, which may then look incomplete. If using a binder, select one with a clear plastic covering on the front. This plastic pocket is handy for inserting your cover page and protecting it during use.

Use clear plastic sheet protectors for your samples. These are three-hole-punched and can be single or connected. See your local office supply store for various types of sheet protectors. You may also want to use tab dividers. Check out the several varieties at your local store with binder in hand. If using sheet protectors, you may need to use extra-wide tabs. When-ever possible, affix a typed label to your tabs rather than writing them by hand. Other optional supplies include photo sheet protectors, pouches for videotapes or other bulky items, and disk or CD holders.

Assembly Steps

After purchasing the supply items, you are ready to put them all together. Following are a few easy steps to follow:

1. Create your sections with your tab dividers and label them.
2. Insert the appropriate materials in sheet protectors and place them in the binder according to the table of contents and tabs.
3. Insert other pages including the cover page, table of contents, section cover pages, and sample overviews.
4. Proofread the portfolio very carefully, page by page and tab by tab, and correct all errors.
5. Review your portfolio with a family member, friend, or colleague who can give it a useful critique.

TIPS FOR INCREASING YOUR PORTFOLIO'S IMPACT

Increase Visual Content

Experts in electronic graphic design recommend that visual information make up a good portion of the pages and screens in electronic media. Some documents may have up to half of the information in some sort of visual form, including blank or white space used around text and graphics.

Create a Visual Identity

Symbols, logos, lines, and other visual elements repeated throughout a document, or the entire portfolio itself, give your portfolio a visual identity. Visual identity ties the various pieces of your portfolio together, making it easier to follow and understand, and giving it a unique personality, while creating a finished, professional look.

Keep Formatting Consistent

Always use a consistent format for all visual elements throughout a document. For example, if you use certain dashes or lines to separate items on one page, you should use them as appropriate on other pages. This creates unity in your document.

Remember That Less Is More

Presenting too much information—whether it's too many samples, too many photos on one page, too much solid text, or too many lines and symbols—clutters your presentation and your message. It is better for a potential employer to remember a few key points and examples than to remember very little because there was too much to see.

Now, sit back and admire your work! You have put together a tool for your job search that is sure to impress any employer and may be just the edge you need to secure that job offer.

ELECTRONIC PORTFOLIOS

In this day and age of web and Internet use by employers and job seekers alike, it might be useful to have an electronic portfolio as another marketing tool. What is an electronic portfolio? This is a personalized, career-oriented website placed on the web to be accessed by others. Electronic portfolios should not take the place of paper-based, hard copy portfolios, however. They are merely another dimension of self-marketing.

If you want to have an electronic portfolio, you must (a) be talented enough to do it yourself, or (b) pay someone to do it for you. You must also have space with an Internet service provider to house your portfolio file and make it available to others.

Advantages

Some advantages of electronic portfolios are as follows:

1. It allows employers to look at your material at their convenience.
2. It allows employers to spend more time reviewing your qualifications outside the interview setting.
3. It allows employers to conveniently share your portfolio with others.
4. It is easy to update by deleting, adding, or changing electronic materials or links quickly. Here is where an electronic portfolio is more flexible than paper-based portfolios—changes can be made in minutes.
5. It is a medium that is colourful, creative, and dynamic in its presentation and can include audio and video clips as well as hyperlinked information.
6. It shows that you are a computer-savvy person who uses current technology in your job search.
7. It is fun to put together!

An electronic portfolio is a high-tech way to let people know who you are, what you can do, and that you are available for work. Physically, it doesn't have to look very different from a paper-based portfolio; the contents can essentially be the same. However, because electronic portfolios, through hyperlinks, have no limit on how much can be displayed, creators of such a tool have the freedom to place much more content online than is practical on paper. Hence a word of caution is appropriate here. Recruiters have limited time to assess portfolios. So, remember to select and include materials that are particularly relevant to the type of employment you are seeking.

Whether you are creating your own online portfolio or are having someone do it for you, you must follow some good formatting, design, and layout rules. The Tips for Increasing Your Portfolio's Impact (page 104) should be reviewed as you develop your online portfolio. In addition, the layout guidelines found on page 107 will help your website look more attractive.

Steps to Create an Electronic Portfolio

Here are a few simple steps to follow while developing your own electronic marketing piece.

Step 1: Collect

Locate all samples and other documents that you want to include. Hopefully, most of your resources are already in easily converted electronic files. Other pieces that are not already in electronic files will need to be scanned. After scanning any materials, check them for accuracy and correct formatting.

Step 2: Organize

Using your paper-based portfolio as a guide, create a sketch or storyboard of your portfolio site on paper. Remember that a website is not linear. Your sketch should include arrows to create a type of flowchart that shows how a viewer can get to where he or she wants to go from anywhere in the web page. Because you cannot control the order in which viewers look at your pages online, each page or section must stand alone.

Start with the home page of your website. Create buttons, or links, on that page for the major sections of your online portfolio. To make navigating easier, use these same buttons on every page of the site. These are your master navigation tools that allow viewers to get where they want to go at all times. Align these buttons or links across the page top or along the left-hand side.

The portfolio sections come next. Make sure these are well defined. If a section contains a single item like a resumé or goal statement, link them directly to that item. If the section is something like a skill area with many samples, link them to an overview page that lists each sample and links to the sample from there.

Finally, your electronic portfolio will have pages for individual samples. In general, you should place only one sample on a page. However, several smaller or shorter items may be combined on one page. Remember to keep sample pages (as well as all others) relatively short. Most viewers are turned off by long, scrolling pages.

Step 3: Create Your Website

Use a software program to create your site (or use someone's services). Follow good principles for visual presentation by remembering these guidelines:

- Maintain a consistent look across all pages.
- Use short paragraphs.
- Avoid italic or other fancy type; these are hard to read on screen.
- Avoid unnecessary features like blinking buttons or animations with no valid purpose.
- Avoid patterned backgrounds that make the text hard to read.
- Keep most images small and simple for faster loading.
- Don't overload the page with graphics. This is distracting and increases loading time.
- Keep it simple. Strive for a site that is easy to read, easy to navigate, and quick to load.

Step 4: Test Your Site and Find a Host

Test your site on different browsers such as Internet Explorer, Netscape, Safari, and Mozilla Firefox. Show it to friends and ask for critical comments. Revise it as needed. Be sure to proof every element of your site, including text, graphics, headings, buttons, and links. You do not want your site to create a poor impression due to a lack of good proofing and quality assurance!

There are many free or inexpensive ways to set up a website on the Internet. If you already have an Internet service provider (ISP), ask the company if they offer personal web page space as part of your regular Internet access fee. Once a host is found, upload your files and start using your impressive online portfolio.

USING YOUR PORTFOLIO

Your portfolio is one of the most powerful tools you have to market yourself during an interview. It provides evidence to back up what you say about yourself; it helps you respond to a variety of interview questions in a clear, organized, and impressive manner; and it even helps the occasional unskilled interviewer with interview conversation.

When to Mention It

As soon as you are comfortable in an interview discussion, mention that you have brought some materials or samples of your work for review. In some types of interviews, you may have to wait until you approach the question-and-answer portion before referring to your portfolio materials. Use it to demonstrate the

Guidelines for Electronic Portfolio Layout

- Make sure your name and contact information are prominent on your web page. Some individuals are reluctant to post personal information such as an address and telephone number on the Internet. If you are not comfortable doing this, an e-mail address is an acceptable alternative means of contact.

- Put no more than one to three main ideas per screen.

- If you are using photos or other graphics, make sure these are crisp, clear, and easy to follow.

- If you are using colour, make sure it is not too bright or neon. Exceedingly bright colours tire the eyes and don't invite prolonged viewing. Select colours that are compatible and allow for easy reading. For example, light yellow lettering on a white background may combine two of your favourite colours, but this makes reading your text next to impossible! Also avoid using too much black as you might convey too sombre a tone with lots of dark colours.

talents, accomplishments, and skills you are promoting. Don't use it to answer direct questions about your qualifications or skills. First describe what you have done or can do, and then demonstrate it with samples from your portfolio.

Structured versus Unstructured Interview

In a rather structured interview, you can use the portfolio to help answer specific questions. For example, suppose an interviewer asks you for an example of how well you work in teams. You can present a story that shows your teamwork skills and abilities, then follow it up with your samples as a demonstration. If you find yourself in an unstructured interview where the discussion is more casual and unfocused, use the portfolio to talk about yourself in general, giving the recruiter a detailed overview of your goals and accomplishments as they are presented in the portfolio.

Read the Situation

Portfolios can help you really score points during the interview; however, even though you know you have an outstanding marketing piece, not everyone may be as excited about it as you are. You may be in an interview with someone who is not familiar with professional portfolios, or someone who prefers verbal conversation to looking through a binder or at a CD. Although you should always let the interviewer know that you have a portfolio and look for opportunities to use it in an interview, never force it on anyone.

Leaving Samples

On the other hand, if you have a recruiter who is really impressed by your portfolio and wants to keep it for a week or so, be careful. You can leave it with her if you do not have any interviews scheduled or on the horizon during that time frame; however, be wary of letting people have your portfolio for an extended time during your job search. Make sure you set up a specific time that you will return to pick it up, usually not more than 24 hours. You don't want such an important marketing tool out of your possession for very long. What you can do to create a memorable impression is offer to leave behind photocopies of appropriate samples that the recruiter may keep. This technique shows you are prepared and leaves a lasting impression of you long after the interview is over. You may keep extra copies of key documents behind the original in your page protectors or have an extra copy of several documents in a small folder to leave behind.

A good portfolio can help you during your job search and later in your career as well. After you begin your career, don't throw it away or bury it at the bottom of some drawer or closet! A portfolio can be the centrepiece of your ongoing career development. Continue to update it with information, material, samples, and letters from your current and future employment. Your professional portfolio can be especially useful during performance reviews, consideration for special projects, and interviews for promotions. By making your portfolio a part of your ongoing career development, you will be prepared to meet challenges and changes that are so much a part of the work world of today.

A professional portfolio is the epitome of marketing yourself!

MY Focus   ESPECIALLY FOR COLLEGE STUDENTS

Several of the benefits to developing a portfolio may not be as obvious as others. Clearly, a portfolio is useful for demonstrating personal skills, talents, and achievements. But did you know that developing this tool assists with your personal assessment and self-promotion from the moment you decide to create one?

BENEFITS

1. Portfolio development requires that you reflect on just how you intend to market yourself.

2. Portfolio development forces you to verbalize your past talents, skills, achievements, and future goals.

3. Portfolio development allows you to reflect back on some of your best work and shining moments, and bring that positive history to today's job search.

4. Portfolios give you a chance to be creative in showing a prospective employer exactly who you are and what you can do.

FINDING YOUR FOCUS

1. Brainstorm for a few moments and come up with a list of five work samples you could use in your professional portfolio. For each sample, indicate the skills and abilities that are reflected.

2. List two of the five visual perception tips discussed in this chapter that you want to keep in mind when you develop your own portfolio.

3. What is another source of visual graphics that you can use in your portfolio besides standard clip art?

4. What are some advantages and disadvantages of the electronic portfolio?

5. Describe two interview scenarios where you could easily refer to your professional portfolio.

CHAPTER

Before the Interview

After completing this chapter, you will be able to:

• Summarize the importance of doing company research.

• Identify the three basic types of interviews.

• Describe the forms of interviews.

• Appreciate the importance of dressing for interview success, and identify appropriate dress and grooming for formal interviews.

How Best to Prepare?

You can succeed if others do not believe in you. But you cannot succeed if you do not believe in yourself.

—DR. SIDNEY NEWTON BREMER

In addition to a well-crafted resumé, interviewing successfully is crucial to your job search. The resumé lets people know who you are and helps you set up an interview. However, the interview is the key that will help unlock the door to the job you want. An interview provides the opportunity to personally present your qualifications and experience to an interviewer. More important, though, is the interviewer's assessment of your personality, interpersonal and communication skills, and ability to fit into the organization. Therefore, it is critical that you convince the recruiter not only of your technical ability to do the job, but also of your personal abilities—you are a good person, you communicate well, and you can fit into and be an asset to the organization.

A recruiter is not merely interested in a list of your courses, degrees, previous or current work experience, or other resumé items. A prospective employer wants a qualified employee who is a team player, can communicate, can take advantage of opportunities, has a high energy level, keeps an upbeat attitude, and demonstrates high ethical standards. That's quite a list of desirable traits! But ultimately, companies want only the best and will do all they can to hire the best candidate. Your challenge is to convince the recruiter that you are the very best person for the job. The setting for this persuasive discussion is, of course, the interview. The interview is one of the most important business meetings you will ever have.

So, how do you prepare for it? This chapter discusses company research and its benefits, the types and forms of interviews, an overview of the stages of an interview, and dressing for interview success.

COMPANY RESEARCH

How many job seekers do thorough company research as part of their interviewing preparation or as part of the preparation for their job search in general? Although it's hard to say what percentage of seekers do a good job researching, it is safe to say that very few engage in this very important activity. Is researching a company really that important? You bet it is! Job-search experts often mention the importance of researching a company before going to an interview, and they also recommend that the research be done before sending out resumés and cover letters. Companies should be researched as part of each job-search process.

The Benefits of Company Research

What are the benefits of researching a company? Many job hunters select potential employers somewhat haphazardly. They may learn about openings through friends, in the classified sections in newspapers, or on the Internet. These job seekers may do a bit of research on a company once an interview is secured, but they are missing out on many benefits by not focusing on a comprehensive plan to research important companies throughout the job-search process. Researching companies helps you select which ones to pursue for employment, create good resumés and cover letters, conduct more effective interviews, and make informed employment decisions.

Research companies for which you are interested in working. These are the companies that will be prime candidates to receive your cover letters and resumés. Learn as much as you can about them including such things as reputation, organizational structure and operation, finances, locations, and current employees. Use this information to determine which ones are good employment matches for you and where you would fit in best.

After you receive a job offer, or even when you are comparing two companies for possible employment, reflect on what you have learned about these companies through the interview process and through your personal research. This information is valuable in helping to determine with whom you will accept employment. As you can see, company research offers benefits throughout the job-search process, but the area that deserves the most focus here is how it relates to the job interview.

Company Research and Interviews

How can company research affect the outcome of an interview? Based on what you learn when you do your research, you will be able to:

- Respond to certain interview questions in a way that demonstrates the fit between your background and the company's needs.
- Skilfully interject a thought or idea about the company that you learned from a recent news story or an online review or evaluation of the firm.
- Ask intelligent questions about the company's corporate philosophy, marketing efforts, or future plans.
- Comment on the firm's mission statement or vision statement and discuss how that relates to the contributions you plan to make to the company.

Using company research in an interview demonstrates to the potential employer that you care enough about the interview and the position to do your homework. Also, when you ask questions about the organization as a whole and your role within it, you demonstrate to the recruiter that you can think beyond the open position and the typical questions about job duties, benefits, and so on. You are proving that you are a person with vision, and you are interested in helping the organization reach its goals. Using company information during an interview can only help you score points with the recruiter.

WHAT SHOULD BE INVESTIGATED?

Now, let's take a look at what should be investigated. Both traditional and electronic sources can supply a wealth of information. In fact, often it is difficult to distinguish between what may be valuable for you to learn and what may be interesting to know but not necessarily useful for your job search.

Certainly you'll want to learn about the company's products or services and their finances; however, it may not be essential for you to learn that the company was founded in a garage by two young entrepreneurs or that the company has had 12 acquisitions in its 50-year history. This may be interesting information but might not be critical during an interview discussion.

On the other hand, it may be useful to learn what percent of their profit is returned to the company to fund research or where the company stands on the list of top performers in the province. It also may be useful for you to demonstrate that you know about a new product, service, or marketing plan that the company has just announced, or to make a comment about an Internet stock analyst who feels that this is the up and coming company in its field.

The exact type of information to be gathered and studied is up to you. Make a list of the information you feel is important. To assist you, the box below offers examples of useful company research information.

Company Research Information

- Products and/or services (current and future)
- Parent company and subsidiaries and their locations
- Number of employees
- Annual sales and/or profits for the last several years
- Potential for growth of the firm and of its industry as a whole
- Position in the industry; major competitors*
- Organizational structure and management style or philosophy
- Corporate mission or vision statement
- Philosophy on training, development, tuition assistance, and other employee programs
- Recent news stories about the firm (expansion, new contract, recent acquisition, new product line)

*Getting competitor information can help you find companies in the same field who may also be potential employers.

GATHERING INFORMATION

One way to gather information is through traditional sources, namely paper-based sources that are most often found in libraries and learning resource centres. Whether you are searching through a business, college, or community library, there are a variety of sources in the reference section, including directories of company information with helpful geographical or industry indexes. Whatever resource books you choose to use, look first at the beginning of the books to familiarize yourself with how they are organized. Also look through the indexes; they can quickly tell you whether the information you want is there. Some examples of these resources are job almanacs, company directories, company annual reports, and employment guides. Also, if a company is small or regional, try going to the public library in the town or city where the company is located. That library may keep files on local companies that contain information not available elsewhere.

A more popular way to research companies is by using *electronic sources* through the Internet. There is often a wealth of information online, including company websites, company directories, and investment web pages.

There are also many different approaches to doing company research online. If you are a current college student or have access to your neighbourhood library, you may be able to search selected databases that contain company information. For instance, some databases provide the full text of thousands of magazine, newspaper, and journal articles—a valuable unbiased source of information about companies. Examples of these databases include CBCA Business, Canadian Newsstand, and Canadian Reference Centre. They provide in-depth reports about public and private companies. Talk to your librarian to see which databases are available and how they can best be explored.

Another approach to researching companies online is searching the Internet using popular search engines such as Yahoo! and Google. Keep in mind that when you do a general search like this, you are likely to get back much more than you expected. Unless you carefully limit your search terms, you will probably have more hits than you have time to review.

Most companies today have a presence on the web. It's sometimes possible to find these pages by entering the name of the company or an abbreviation of its name followed by a period and the term "com" into your browser's address space—i.e., xyzcompany.com. If this doesn't work, go back to the search engine and try the name there as a search term. Remember, when you explore a company's website you are finding only what the company wants you to learn about it. Typical website information includes products and services offered, corporate mission statements, division or branch offices, financial information, a list of staff with e-mail addresses, and even current job openings! Although this is useful in your job search, it shouldn't be your only means of gathering company information.

Another very effective way to learn about companies is through other people or *personal sources*. Using your networking contacts, get the names of people who are employed with the companies in which you are interested and make arrangements to talk to these people. Alert your family, friends, and acquaintances to the companies in which you are interested and see if they know an employee or someone who has a connection to these companies.

Another excellent method of gathering research information through other people is scheduling informational interviews with persons employed by various companies. Human Resources staff and hiring authorities, as well as your various personal contacts, can help set up these informational interviews. When participating in informational interviews, having a comprehensive list of questions is very useful. See Chapter 3 for examples of these questions.

Finally, if you are a soon-to-be college graduate, you have a very useful resource at your fingertips: your college career services department. In many schools, this department contains an extremely knowledgeable group of people who can assist you in everything from resumé advice, to interviewing, to information on job openings. Some departments may have useful information on national, regional, and local companies.

PREPARATION: THE KEY TO INTERVIEW SUCCESS

Like anything else that you want to become successful in, interviewing requires planning and preparation. Review the following points to help you prepare for a successful interview.

Find out as much as you can about the position. If you have applied for it, you already know the basics, but try to find out more. Call the company's human resources department and tell them you will be interviewing for a certain position. Ask them to give you a further description of the job and its requirements. After you have a good view of the position, relate your own background and abilities to it point by point in your own mind. This comparison will be quite useful later on in the interview.

Be aware of typical interview questions and practise your answers out loud. Study lists of interview questions and rehearse your responses out loud. Keep in mind how you want to answer these, but don't try to memorize any answers. Remember that talking always sounds better in your head but it is crucial to practise out loud so you become comfortable selling your qualifications and skills.

Prepare a list of questions for the employer to answer. After you've researched the company, you'll probably still have questions. (Questions about the job itself are addressed in the next chapter.)

Have an idea of what the competitive salary is for the position and know your own salary requirements. Sometimes it's not easy to learn about salaries. If you cannot get information on a particular position in a firm, at least have an idea of what the going rate is for someone who had the amount of training and experience necessary to fill the position. Professional associations, professional periodicals, college career centres, and other resources can be helpful for this information.

Arrange a mock interview. This is one of the most positive things you can do to prepare for your interview. Most college and university career centres offer mock interviews. Very few students actually take advantage of this service; however, when they do, it is a valuable experience for them. In most cases candidates do not answer the first few questions well at all. Think about this: in a real interview you cannot afford a warm-up period. A mock interview gives you the opportunity to get constructive feedback on your interviewing skills and an opportunity to correct your errors, or at the very least make sure that you're on the right track.

Check to see whether your school subscribes to Optimal Resume or another similar program. Optimal Resume is a website that has tools to assist you with creating your resumé, cover letters, online portfolio, and interview component. The interview component is one of the best interactive tools to help you prepare for your interview. Using this tool, you can select your interviewer and the type of interview questions you want to be asked. If you have a webcam you can record your answers and play them back. This site even has a "coach" button to assist you if you are unsure how to answer the question.

Increase Confidence

The most important thing that will happen to you with all of your advance preparation is that you will increase your level of confidence going into the interview. That alone is well worth the work you have done. If you can increase your confidence you will do a better job of selling yourself. Above all, remember: it is not always the most qualified candidate who secures the position but the candidate who does the best job of selling himself or herself.

TYPES OF INTERVIEWS

Interviews may be one of several types and take one of several forms. When you know what to expect—when you determine the nature of the interview—you'll be able to prepare properly for any interview. The three basic types of interviews are:

- referral interview
- screening interview
- selection interview

Referral Interview

A *referral interview* gives the employer a chance to look at you for future reference. This could be the result of networking, developing a meeting through common contacts, or even a chance meeting at a professional society event. Sometimes a referral interview may open the door to a job opportunity before it is advertised. In any case, a referral interview can put you in touch with valuable contacts. Although an informational interview is not by nature a referral interview, when you have an informational interview, the interviewer may keep you and your resumé in mind for any future openings.

Screening Interview

The purpose of a *screening interview* is to enable an employer to narrow the field of applicants. The interviewer reviews your qualifications to find reasons to accept or reject your candidacy. When this type of interview is scheduled, it is often conducted by human resource personnel. Your best approach during a screening interview is to follow the interviewer's lead. Keep your responses concise, but remember, this may be the only chance you have to sell yourself. The screening interview is typically the beginning of the path to a job offer. If, after the interview, the human resources person likes you and feels you are qualified for the position, then you may go on to the selection interview.

Selection Interview

The *selection interview* is the type of interview that a department head, supervisor, or other hiring authority conducts. This is when a candidate typically meets the person who will ultimately make the hiring decision. During this interview, the interviewer tries to determine from your answers, past experience, and attitudes whether you're right for the organization and the position. By noting how you listen, think, and express yourself, the interviewer can decide whether you are likely to get along with others in the organization. This interview process usually ends in a hiring decision.

Your best approach during a selection interview is to show interest in the job, relate your training and experience to the company's needs, listen attentively, and display enthusiasm. The stages of a typical selection interview are discussed later. Keep in mind that you must always sell yourself and your skills.

FORMS OF INTERVIEWS

Now, let's take a look at the various forms an interview can take. They are: directed, unstructured, stress, panel, group, telephone, and video conferencing.

Directed Interview

The *directed interview* form, generally used for the screening interview, is highly organized from start to finish. Often working from a checklist or script, the recruiter asks a series of questions within a specific time period. Your answers are noted in writing and often scored. The directed interview form also can be used during the selection interview. This type of interview can be conducted one-on-one or by a panel. It is interesting to note that some directed interviewing may be done over the telephone.

Unstructured Interview

By contrast, the less formal *unstructured interview* has an open and relaxed feel. By posing broad questions, the interviewer encourages you to talk (but be careful: you don't want to get too relaxed and divulge more than you should). Used in some selection interview situations, this form of interviewing provides you with an opportunity to bring out your unique personality and demonstrate that you are the best person for the position. Ensure that you cover all of the reasons why you are the best person for the job. Some selection interviews may include both the directed and unstructured formats.

Stress Interview

The unstructured form is quite the opposite of the *stress interview* form. This approach intentionally puts you under stress to observe your reactions. For the unsuspecting applicant, the experience can be unsettling. Stress interviews consist of pointed questions designed to cause you difficulty when responding. This type of questioning is challenging and can lead to feeling defensive. The best way to handle this form of interview is to remain calm and try to concisely, but accurately, answer questions put to you. A stress interview may be conducted by one person or a group of people.

Panel Interview

The next format for an interview is the *panel interview* form, a most challenging interview situation. A panel interview usually will be conducted by two to five interviewers. Everyone there will ask questions. The problem some candidates have is they don't know with whom they should maintain eye contact when answering. Always start at the person who asked the question and then look at the others while giving your answer, but remember to return your attention back to the person who posed the question before you finish your answer.

Group Interview

The *group interview* is another growing trend. Sometimes it consists of two candidates interviewing with one interviewer at the same time. Both of you hear the interviewer's questions and the other candidate's responses. You really need to concentrate on yourself and not get wrapped up in what the other candidate is saying. You are not just competing against the other candidate that you see but all the other candidates, just as in any other interview. Sometimes this sort of interview is even more of a group situation, where a number of candidates are present in a room and must solve some problems by working together. Often employers use this type of interview for selecting staff to work in a team environment. The employer is more often looking for team players, not necessarily for leaders. If this is the case, you and the other applicants must work together accordingly.

Telephone Interview

Another interview format is the *telephone interview*. It has been reported that many recruiters are now using the telephone more than ever before. A recruiter or human resource professional may use a phone call to make the first contact with the candidate. Oftentimes, questions are asked to confirm the candidate's qualifications or to present additional details about the job before a regular, on-site interview is conducted. When receiving these calls, strive to be at your sharpest. This is challenging as you may not know when the calls will occur.

Here are some tips for successful telephone interviews. Remember, your goal is to pass this phone interview so that you can make it to the face-to-face interview. When a call like this arrives, snap yourself into a professional interview mode and adopt a businesslike manner. Have an organized place where you can take career-related phone calls. Ideally, this is a room where you can close the door. In this area, you should have all of the necessary materials—resumé, company information, and a list of questions to ask the interviewer. When on the phone, remember: no eating, drinking, or smoking. These activities are magnified over telephone lines. Take notes and use your prepared questions. Avoid yes-or-no answers. Remember, you need to shine during the phone interview. So, take the opportunities to elaborate on your answers or add information that can help sell you. Finally, take surprise calls in stride. If you have prepared for phone interviews, unexpected calls won't be such a surprise. Try to improve with each one you complete.

Video Conferencing Interview

Video conferencing interviews will continue to gain in popularity. This type of interview can be more cost efficient for major companies when interviewing out-of-town candidates and has many of the benefits of a personal interview. Employers can get a good idea of your personality, body language, appearance, and conversation style. You can make the most of this type of interview by being prepared for it. Dress conservatively in solid colours. Be prepared to experience time lags and allow for the delay when speaking. Look straight at the camera as if it were a person. The camera will magnify movements you make so be careful not to use your hands to make a point. If there are problems with the sound or picture, make sure you advise the interviewer.

INTERVIEW STAGES

No one can say how long an interview will last. Certainly, a very short interview is not a good sign; conversely, a longer interview is more promising. Interviews can last from 15 minutes to most of the day if they are conducted by several people. A day-long or half-day interview really consists of several shorter interviews, but may feel like one huge one! The following interview stages are discussed in detail in the next chapter: pre-visit, greeting/small talk, presentation of company and position, resumé review, questions and answers (interviewer and applicant), answering final questions from applicant, closing, and follow-up.

DRESSING FOR INTERVIEW SUCCESS

A discussion of what happens before the interview is not complete without talking about dressing for interview success. In an interview, your attire plays a supporting role. Appropriate attire supports your image as a person who is a serious candidate, one who understands the nature of the industry in which he is trying to become employed. There is a specific level of dress appropriateness: not casual, not business casual, and not formal or dressy. It is a professional style that compliments the wearer and is appropriate for greeting clients. Stay away from the temptation to dress down. Even if the employees at the firm dress quite casually, dress a notch above that.

Attire Guidelines

Here are some attire guidelines for both men and women:

- A two-piece, matched suit is always the best and safest choice.
- Stick with conservative colours such as navy, dark grey, and black.
- Solids or a subtle weave fabric is best
- Make sure the suit fits you properly.

- Seek professional help at the store on the best style, colour, and fit for you.
- One good quality suit is sufficient; you don't need to buy two if you can't afford them.
- Vary your look with different shirts and ties or blouses.
- Everything you wear must be clean and pressed, with all tags and dangling threads removed.

Specifics for Men

There are exceptions: in interviews for student internships or for part-time employment, such professional attire may not be necessary and business casual may be acceptable. Your research may help you determine what is appropriate and, if in doubt, a more professional look will score more points than a casual one.

- Remember to select conservative ties.
- Shirts should be long-sleeved, even in summer.
- Some people believe that a white shirt conveys honesty and intelligence.
- Socks should be dress socks and complement the suit colour.
- Shoes should be leather.
- Your belt should match the shoe colour.
- Wear a conservative watch and very little other jewellery.
- Remove earrings or piercings before the interview.

Specifics for Women

There is some question as to the most appropriate type of suit for an interview: skirt or dress pants. Some recruiters feel that skirts are more appropriate for interviews, while others say that dress pants are fine. If you choose to wear a skirt, don't purchase that piece of clothing until you sit in it facing a mirror. That is what the interviewer will see.

- Skirts should have a conservative hemline and fit.
- Small slits in skirts are fine; large slits are inappropriate.
- Dress pants should be creased or tailored and not tight or flowing.
- A tailored blouse or top should be worn underneath the suit jacket.
- The colour and print should coordinate with the suit colour.
- Blouses or tops should not be cut lower than neckline.
- Shoes should match the suit colour.
- Choose closed-toe pumps and avoid extreme heels.
- Shoes should be comfortable (if you don't usually wear heels this is not the time to try them out).
- Hosiery should be plain and sheer in neutral colours that complement the suit.
- Jewellery should be conservative and simple.
- Cosmetics should also be simple and appropriate.
- Nails should be well groomed.
- If you carry a purse, keep it small and simple. Purse colour should coordinate with shoes.

Some Examples

Standard Interview Attire for Women—with skirt

Standard Interview Attire for Women— with pants

Standard Interview Attire for Men

Alternative Interview Attire: Men—no tie, Women—no jacket

Alternative Interview Attire for Men—no jacket

Grooming

Good grooming is important for both men and women.

- Hair should be clean, neat, and out of the face.
- Men choosing to have facial hair should make sure it is well groomed, too.
- Polish your shoes and make sure the heels are in good repair.
- Check your clothing for missing buttons, lint, and pet hair.
- Perfume or cologne should not be worn.
- Make sure you do not smell like smoke, garlic, onions, or any foreign scent.
- Remove any obvious facial piercings.

Image

It's been said that you never get a second chance to make a first impression; your appearance and the way you present yourself are crucial. The image you project in the interview is critical to getting the job, and once you get the job, that image will then be important in the workplace each and every day. For further advice on professional attire and image, there are books and magazine articles that discuss the current advice for working (and interviewing) professionals.

As you can see, there are many important issues to consider before the interview. The next chapter discusses the important points of the interview itself.

MY Focus — ESPECIALLY FOR COLLEGE STUDENTS

A very important part of marketing yourself successfully, whether during your job search or after you have gotten the job, is dressing appropriately. Although dress codes on the job tend to be more casual today and current trends in personal dress and style also tend to be casual, don't underestimate the power of a professional look. The adage "the clothes make the man (or woman)" really is true. As you are getting ready to market yourself, walk into your closet, take a long, hard look, and assess the following:

- suits/dresses for interviewing
- coordinating shirts for business suits
- conservative ties
- socks or hose to be worn with suit/dress
- dress shoes that are in good repair
- formal winter or trench coat as appropriate
- appropriate watch and limited jewellery

Have at least two interview outfits. Also, before you purchase anything to supplement your interviewing clothing, seek professional advice:

- Go to a local, upscale department or clothing store that has a knowledgeable staff to assist with clothing selection.
- Indicate what you are looking for and ask for advice.
- Take a look at item samples.
- Purchase items of the best quality you can afford, because inexpensive clothing may not give you the professional look you need to make the very best impression.

FINDING YOUR FOCUS

1. Select one or two of your top companies and research them. Use print materials, electronic resources, and personal or telephone interviews. Collect the information in a file for use later.

2. Write a brief list of questions you believe might be part of both a directed interview and an unstructured interview.

3. Have a friend call you and role-play a telephone interview. Notice how your posture, facial expression, and environment influence your performance. Evaluate the best places to receive telephone interview calls and go to that place when you are called. (Tip: Although many people today take most of their calls on cell phones, be very careful about participating in telephone interviews in a setting that is not quiet and conducive to a professional business discussion.)

4. Discuss with a friend different forms of interviews you have each experienced. Share the positives and negatives of each form of interview.

CHAPTER 9

During and After the Interview

CHAPTER OBJECTIVES

After completing this chapter, you will be able to:

- Describe the various interview stages.

- Distinguish between standard and behavioural interview questions.

- Effectively respond to a variety of interview questions.

- Construct effective proof stories for interviews.

- Ask general, defining, and controlling questions during the interview.

- Use your portfolio effectively during an interview.

- Apply basic dining etiquette during interview and career situations.

- Distinguish types of interview testing, and prepare for them.

Being the Strongest Candidate

In the middle of difficulty lies opportunity.

—ALBERT EINSTEIN

Now that you are prepared for the interview, let's take a look at some important aspects of the interview itself. This chapter discusses the interview stages (mentioned briefly in the previous chapter), interview questions (both the ones you answer and the ones you should ask), portfolio use, etiquette, testing, negotiating, and thank-yous. It also explores some key points on following up after the interview and some ideas to keep in mind as you move into the decision-making process that occurs after the offer.

Let's look at each of the interview steps in detail. The following discussion uses a typical interview format as an example, but remember that there may be individuals who conduct their interviews in a different manner or different order.

STAGES OF THE INTERVIEW

Pre-Visit

This is a stage that actually happens before the day of the interview. Many interviews take candidates to unfamiliar cities, towns, or neighbourhoods. Because you don't want any surprises the day of your interview, it is recommended that you conduct a pre-visit to the location where the interview will take place. On the pre-visit, leave at the same time you plan to leave on the day of the interview to see how long it takes to arrive. Note any factors that could cause delays (e.g., railroad crossings or particularly heavy traffic areas). A pre-visit also ensures that you will know exactly how to get to the facility on interview day.

After arriving at the company, walk into the building and look around. If the lobby has a security presence, go up to the desk and let them know what you are doing. Some companies will not let outsiders into their facility without an approved identification or a security pass. Ask about security requirements when you are asked to come for the interview. Looking around the company's lobby or central area gives you a feel for things. Observe the employees as they come and go and note how they are dressed. If you are familiar with the location, you will be more comfortable on the interview day. So, whenever you can, try to make a pre-visit.

Greeting/Small Talk

The first stage of the interview day consists of greeting/small talk. This stage and its first two activities happen shortly after you arrive. The greeting occurs when your interviewer arrives and greets you, often shaking your hand. First impressions are made by both parties during the greeting. These impressions are based on appearance and actions. You should make the strongest first impression possible. Be prepared to give a firm handshake and a great smile, and look the recruiter directly in the eyes. When shaking hands, a firm meeting of the hands with one or two shakes is appropriate. By custom, the interviewer should extend his hand first. If this doesn't happen, extend your hand. After you arrive at the location where the interview will take place, it's time for the small talk.

Everyone knows what small talk is, but why is there a stage in the interview dedicated to this? Actually, small talk is relatively important. During this time, first impressions continue to be made, the recruiter attempts to help the candidate feel at ease, and the candidate starts to relax and prepare for the next interview stage. Although you should not hesitate to be friendly and somewhat spontaneous during this phase, remember that you are being evaluated *all* of the time. Follow the recruiter's lead regarding topics for this light conversation. Sit in the middle of the chair (don't lean back in a more casual pose) and tilt your upper body slightly forward to indicate engagement and an interest in what is going on.

Presentation of Company/Position

It is quite common for recruiters (especially human resource personnel who may be conducting the initial screening interview) to provide an overview of the company and the position at this point. Listen closely and ask questions when appropriate. This is often a good time to work into the conversation something you already know about the company from your previous research. When the job is discussed, ask a few questions now, but save other questions until after the particulars of the position have been described.

Resumé Review

At this point, the interviewer refreshes himself about your candidacy by scanning your resumé. Be keenly aware of what you said about yourself on your resumé. During this phase, or later during the question-and-answer phase, the interviewer may ask you questions about key information found in the resumé. It may take several minutes for him or her to reread your resumé, and this quiet time can be a bit unsettling. Avoid the temptation to start justifying or clarifying anything on your resumé. Simply wait for any questions about your resumé or for the next phase of the interview to begin.

Questions and Answers

This stage is when the meeting turns into an actual business situation. Now it is time to get down to business—the business of hiring. There are a variety of questions that will be asked of you and some that you will ask the interviewer. These questions are discussed in detail later in this chapter.

Closing

Signs that you are coming to the end of the interview include a slowing of the questioning or rhythm of the interview, a glance at a watch, a request for any additional questions, or a statement that the recruiter will contact you. As you

approach the interview end, remember, it's never too late to make a negative impression. Don't let your guard down. Keep a professional image, keep your energy level up, and look positive and eager.

The interview ends when loose ends are wrapped up. Is there anything you need clarification on? Anything you feel should have been mentioned and wasn't? (Be careful here with issues of salary. Don't talk about it unless the interviewer brings it up. More on salary issues in the negotiating discussion in Chapter 10.)

Don't leave the interview without finding out:

- What happens next.
- When it is expected to happen.
- If the recruiter says that he will call you, ask, "When might I expect that call?"
- If the recruiter is not sure when, ask if you can call in a few days or a week to find out what decisions have been made.
- Ask for the recruiter's business card and make sure you make the call!

Actively following up the interview puts more of your job search in your hands. If you leave the interview not knowing what the next step is and when it will occur, all you can do is wait for the phone to ring.

Final Sell

It is extremely important at this point, if you haven't done this already, to make sure that the interviewer is aware of your interest in the position. Make sure you thank him or her and restate your interest before leaving. This final sell on your part can make the difference in getting the job offer.

Now that you are familiar with the typical interview stages, the discussion turns to the question-and-answer session.

QUESTIONS ASKED DURING THE INTERVIEW

As mentioned briefly in Chapter 8, you should be aware of and prepare for questions you will be asked during the interview. You also must consider what questions you want answered during the interview. Keep in mind that the question-and-answer stage is when the most information is exchanged, and when first impressions give way to an overall impression and opinion of the candidate.

Let's look at the two basic interview question categories—standard questions and behaviour-based questions—and types of questions in each category. We'll examine the standard questions first.

Standard Questions

Although the actual questions asked will vary with the interviewer, the following questions are usually asked:

1. Can you tell me something about yourself?

_____

_____

_____

2. Why should I hire you?

_____

_____

_____

3. What are your strengths?

_____

_____

_____

4. What are your weaknesses?

_____

_____

_____

5. Why are you applying for this position?

_____

_____

_____

6. How are you qualified for this position?

_____

_____

_____

7. Why are you interested in working for our firm?

_____

_____

_____

8. What can you contribute to this company?

_____

_____

_____

9. What are your short-term goals?

_____

_____

_____

10. What are your long-term goals?

_____

_____

_____

As you read the above questions, complete the best answers for your own situation. Here are a few tips to keep in mind when asked some of these questions.

Question 1: Can you tell me something about yourself? When asking this question, most interviewers are interested not only in what you tell them but also in how you respond to the question. The best advice for answering this question: do not give too much information. Keep your response to the point. The worst way to respond is to ramble on about your childhood, high school, previous jobs, and so on.

Focus your answer on the situation at hand. Start with information that qualifies you for the job. Mention skills, traits, employment, and education that make you right for the position and prove that you are a good match for the job. By responding this way, you haven't missed out on an opportunity to sell yourself for the position. Thus, instead of going on about the paper route or high school sports achievement you are so proud of, you are starting off the interview by selling yourself. And after all, isn't that why you are there?

Questions 3 and 4: What are your strengths and weaknesses? Recruiters are just as interested in how prepared you are to answer this question as they are in what you actually say. When preparing to respond, reflect on and write down just what your job-related strengths and weaknesses are. Then, re-examine your list and decide which ones you can talk about. Are you particularly good at working under stress? Can you multi-task well? Are you a good group leader or member?

Regarding your weaknesses, use some that are not too critical. For example, maybe you are a perfectionist and sometimes that causes you to take a little longer with a project than you should, or maybe public speaking is not your cup of tea. Whatever weakness you choose to discuss, it is imperative that you finish by saying something positive. For example, if you have these perfectionist tendencies, explain that you are working on not being so concerned with every minor detail so you can finish assignments on time.

Questions 9 and 10: What are your short-term and long-term goals? Here the interviewer is interested in your future professional goals. Interviewers want to learn if you are a person with vision, if you are someone who has plans and knows how to make those plans into realities. Typically, when asking about short-term goals, interviewers want to know where you see yourself professionally in five years. For long-term goals, they want to know about your professional plans 10 years down the road.

Sometimes answering these questions is difficult, especially for candidates who are seeking their first entry-level position and don't have experience in their chosen fields yet. In response, talk about the positions you'd like to hold in the future or the professional responsibilities you would like to have. Discuss the future training and education you plan to obtain. Entry-level candidate or not, you should put some thought into how you will respond.

Behaviour-Based Questions

Behaviour-based questions are now quite common and important in the interview process. These structured questions require the candidate to apply knowledge, skills, and abilities to specific situation-related questions. The questions probe a candidate's past behaviour in situations similar to those encountered in the job. A candidate's responses tell the interviewer something about the candidate's specific reactions to past circumstances. Typically, past behaviour is an accurate indicator of future behaviour.

Some of the areas covered by behaviour-based questions include communication skills, supervision experience, analyzing data, dealing with change, self-management, and team building. The box above offers a list of

Sample Behaviour-Based Questions

- Tell me about a difficult situation you dealt with when supervising others. What did you do and what were the results?

- Tell me about a time when you had to collect, manipulate, and analyze data.

- Describe a time when you had to use your best oral communication skills. What was the situation and what was the outcome?

- Describe a time you took an idea or concept and turned it into a program or project.

- Describe a time when you had to adjust to change. How did you cope or adjust to this change?

- Explain a role you filled as a group/team member.

- We all face disappointments in life. Tell me about a time when you had to handle disappointment or rejection.

- Describe a situation that required you to show initiative.

- Tell me about a time when someone made an unreasonable request of you. How did you react and what happened?

- Describe a time when you were most frustrated or discouraged in reaching your objectives or goals. How did it turn out?

- Describe the last time you did something that went beyond what was expected in work or school.

- Tell me about a difficult challenge/problem you've faced and how you handled it.

You will find additional behaviour-based questions organized according to various assessment traits on our **Companion Website**.

behaviour-based questions. Look them over and think about how you might answer them. A more detailed list of behaviour-based questions can be found on the **Companion Website**.

Proof Stories

A very effective technique for dealing with all kinds of interview questions, including behaviour-based ones, is to tell brief stories. We are not referring here to fictional storytelling. Instead, we are referring to telling a story that helps prove the qualities you say you have.

Think about it for a moment. What do most of us like to hear and tend to remember? Stories. Stories are specific, entertaining, and often memorable. You want the interviewer to remember you and your qualifications. An organized, effective story does the job.

Consider this scenario: A campus interviewer just spent the day talking to 15 graduating seniors. All 15 have the same degree, similar qualifications, and similar grade point averages. But one student, Kathy, is remembered more than

the others. When discussing job qualifications, most students said they were dependable, flexible, and good problem solvers. Kathy also mentioned these traits, but she also told brief stories that proved or verified what she was saying about herself. These stories are called proof stories.

Proof stories help you demonstrate specific skills you possess and the employer wants. The skills can be technical (the ability to program in a specific computer language) or transferable (the ability to work independently). Whatever your traits or skills, use proof stories to establish their existence.

How to Create a Proof Story

A proof story takes only a few minutes to tell, relates directly to those traits sought for the position, and has three distinct parts. To develop these stories, review the actions and activities from your past and develop a list of the key traits, skills, and attributes you possess.

Once you've generated your list, identify situations and circumstances that required you to use those traits or skills. For example, if you work well under pressure, use as your proof story an occasion when you successfully worked a double shift during the holiday season. Another example may be a story about a time you used good communication and problem-solving skills to solve a computer problem over the telephone.

Remember, interviewers are more likely to listen to and recall specific stories about specific incidents. Therefore, instead of saying that you work at a hospital emergency room and usually work under pressure, think of a specific evening or time when things were extremely hectic or challenging and speak about that.

Situation/Task, Action, Result (S.T.A.R.)

How do you format a story about a specific incident or situation? It's as simple as 1-2-3, or, more precisely, S-T-A-R. Proof stories are most effectively told in three parts:

- Situation/task
- Action
- Results

First, identify a trait you want a story to demonstrate; for example, working under pressure. Next, determine the situation or task in your story. Where were you? Who were you working for? What situation led you to do something? For example, where were you working and what was your job when you were required to work under pressure? It's not necessary to provide extensive details; just explain enough for the listener to understand the context of the action you will describe.

Next, describe the action you took. Make sure to use appropriate, powerful action words. Using the working under pressure example, perhaps you coordinated a group of people to handle an emergency, or maybe you worked hard and long to debug some code in a computer program that had to be used the next day.

The final part of developing a proof story is the results. This is when you make a strong impression on the interviewer by revealing the results that occurred when you took the action(s) you described earlier in your story.

Continuing with the example of working under pressure, perhaps due to your quick actions and staff coordination, you saved the company thousands of dollars by protecting equipment that was at risk. Or due to your hard work and long hours debugging a program, the product was ready to be shipped to customers on schedule. Telling a simple, focused three- to four-minute proof story provides a specific, memorable demonstration of a skill or trait you profess to have.

Telling a Story

Another way to think of this is to remember that all stories have three parts.

- Beginning (*Situation/Task*)
- Middle (*Action*)
- End (*Result*)

Some people find it easier to create their proof stories by referring to the above terms. The end result must ultimately capture and retain the interest of the listener, in this case the interviewer(s).

Think about two friends who tell stories. The first friend includes a lot of detail and information in the story that literally makes it come to life. You are interested and engaged, you can picture the events and characters in your mind, and are very interested in the outcome of the story. Your second friend, however, leaves out important information, backtracks, and doesn't include much detail. Pretty soon you have lost interest, are thinking about other things, and just want the story to be done.

Now think about the interviewer, who has asked the same question of several other candidates that day. How can you craft your story to capture his or her interest and make it memorable? Details are what make the story interesting, more believable and come to life, so use them to your advantage in order to engage the interviewer(s) in your story.

Following are some proof story examples that show the level of detail and concreteness necessary for these stories to be effective.

Now that you have a basic understanding of proof stories, it's time to develop your own.

Proof Story Worksheet

List below some technical, personal, and transferable skills or traits that would be useful for proof stories.

_____

_____

_____

Use the following format to set up your own proof stories.

Trait or characteristic this story demonstrates: _____

1. *Set up the background to the story.* Briefly describe the situation that called for you to use the skill. Where were you? What led to the situation?

2. *Describe the action that was taken or the response that was given.* Based on the situation above, what happened? What did you do? When and where did you do it? How and why did you do it? This description should contain action verbs that help create a powerful story.

Sample Proof Stories

STORY #1

Characteristics this story demonstrates: clear thinking, leadership skills

Situation/task: One evening when I was the supervisor in charge at an ABC Furniture warehouse, the sprinkler system malfunctioned and water began soaking all of the stock. The sprinklers had been operating for 10 minutes, so we had to move fast to salvage the inventory.

Action: I got on the intercom system and alerted all personnel in the front warehouse area and in the break room. When the workers arrived to help, I arranged them into teams and gave them various tasks: use the lift trucks, move the stock to unaffected areas, and clean up the affected area.

Results: Within three hours, $750,000 worth of furniture had been moved to dry areas and saved from severe water damage. The warehouse facilities were cleaned and the stock was returned to its normal storage area within five hours. The entire staff felt a sense of pride and accomplishment in their efforts.

Other characteristics demonstrated by this story are working well under stress and dedication.

STORY #2

Characteristics this story demonstrates: customer relations skills

Situation/task: I was working as a field service technician for YXZ Electronics company. My job was to troubleshoot and repair electronic copy machines and mail machines. One day, I was dispatched to a law firm where a copy machine was experiencing numerous problems. When I arrived, the office manager met me at the door and started shouting about the equipment's lack of reliability. He also said that he needed to get important documents copied within the hour or there would be serious ramifications.

Action: I listened patiently, and then I asked questions about the nature of the problem and how long it had been occurring. I immediately ran some diagnostic tests, but was still uncertain as to the problem. With the manager hovering over my shoulder, I removed the back panel and discovered a broken program switch was causing the problem. I assured the office manager that the equipment would be up and running within the hour.

Results: After 30 minutes, the copier was operational. Although the copier was no longer under warranty, as a goodwill gesture I did not charge the customer for the service call. The office manager was impressed with my speedy repair, grateful for the billing break, and got his important document copied in time.

Additional characteristics demonstrated by this story are good communication skills and working well under pressure.

Tips for Creating Proof Stories

- Prepare several stories that relate to applicable skills or qualifications before you begin interviewing.

- Don't go into extensive detail in the background section. Reveal just enough detail so the listener can understand the basic story and you capture the attention of the interviewer.

- Don't lump your results statement in with your action discussion. Clearly describe the actions taken. Then, transition to the last part of the story, the results.

- Try to create a story that reflects one specific incident or setting. Stories that are too broad lose impact.

- When you finish your results statement, link the ending of your story back to the trait mentioned at the beginning.

- Use these stories to discuss how you meet various job requirements. Have the interviewer describe the ideal candidate for the position, then prove to her that you are the one using your proof story.

3. *Reveal the results that occurred due to the action taken.* What was the end result? Try to quantify results whenever possible or measure what happened against a standard. Don't hesitate to brag about the results achieved: that's the purpose of the entire proof story.

In relating this story, you may have discovered that it displayed other traits. List them on the lines that follow.

_____

_____

_____

ILLEGAL QUESTIONS

It is important to understand that not all questions employers ask in an interview are legal. It's also important to understand that, when you are asked these questions, there is often more than one way to handle them, but you can't choose the best alternative without some knowledge of illegal questions.

The Canadian Human Rights Act entitles all individuals to equal employment opportunities without regard to the following:

- Race or colour
- National or ethnic origin
- Religion
- Age
- Family/marital status
- Sex
- Pardoned conviction
- Disability
- Sexual orientation

What If You Get Asked an Inappropriate Question?

Most of the time the interviewer is not intentionally asking you an illegal question. Sometimes he or she is trying to put you at ease or trying to learn more about you as a person. Only you can decide at the time what you wish to reveal. While you have several options available to you, they are not all in your best interests, as you will see.

Look at the question behind the question. For example, if an interviewer asks if you are planning on starting a family in the near future, you have a variety of options:

a) You may wish to respond that if hired you will be committed to your position and will perform all the functions of the job. This is your best choice as you have not offended anyone and yet still not provided the illegal information requested.

b) You could say that while starting a family is not in your immediate plans, you haven't ruled it out. Answering this way, however, will likely not be in your best interest, and remember, the interviewer is not allowed to ask you this question.

c) You also have the choice of stating that you are not sure how this question is relevant to your ability to perform the job. Choosing this option will send the message to the interviewer that he or she has overstepped but will likely eliminate you from the selection process.

Illegal questions are not that common with large companies, but you still need to be aware of what your rights are. Remember that only you can ultimately decide how you wish to handle them. For more information you may wish to view the website of the Canadian Human Rights Commission, at www.chrc-ccdp.ca.

INTERVIEW QUESTIONS FOR YOU TO ASK

Not only is it important for you to answer questions well and provide proof stories whenever possible, it is also important that you ask pertinent questions. Remember that an interview should be a dialogue. You should get answers that will help you make sound employment decisions. One of the best ways to learn as much as you can about a company, position, or circumstance is to ask focused questions. Let's divide these questions into three categories: general, defining, and controlling.

General Questions

General questions are asked to obtain useful information for later decision making. Such questions include the following:

1. If I am hired, will there be a formal training program or on-the-job training?
2. What are the expectations of new employees?
3. Is there a probationary period? How long is it?
4. How is an employee evaluated and promoted?
5. If I am hired, who will be my immediate supervisor? Can you tell me about his or her management style?
6. What are the opportunities for personal growth in your company?
7. Describe a typical assignment I might receive.
8. What will I be doing on a daily basis? What is an average day like for someone in this position?
9. How much travel is normally expected with this position?
10. What characteristics does a successful person have in your company?

Illegal Questions

I haven't heard your name before—where are you from?

Where were you born?

Have you ever changed your name?

What was your maiden name?

What is your original language?

Are you a Canadian citizen?

Were you born in Canada?

What is your age?

What is your birth date?

May I see your birth certificate?

Are you married? Engaged? Divorced? Widowed? Married common-law?

Do you plan to have a family? When?

How many children do you have?

Is there a chance your spouse could be transferred?

What are your child-care arrangements?

How tall are you?

How much do you weigh?

Questions about height and weight are not acceptable unless they are genuine occupational requirements.

Do you have any disabilities?

What is the name of your family doctor?

Have you ever received worker's compensation?

Is a counsellor or a therapist currently treating you?

Are you taking any prescribed or recreational drugs?

Do you drink alcohol?

What race are you?

Will you be able to work on [a religious holiday]?

What church do you belong to?

Have you ever been convicted of a crime?

Have you ever been arrested?

Legal Questions

What is your name?

Are you able to read, write, and understand English?

Testing of applicants for language proficiency is allowed where job-related only.

Are you legally entitled to work in Canada?

Do you meet legal age requirements?

Are you over the age of 18?

Would you be willing to relocate?

Are there any circumstances that would prevent you from:

- working overtime?
- overnight travel out of the area?

Are you able to lift 20 kilograms and transfer it 50 metres?

Do you have a condition that could affect your ability to do the job?

Do you have any condition we should consider in our selection?

Offers of employment can be conditional upon successful completion of a medical exam if the employee's condition is related to job duties.

This position requires weekend work. Does this pose a problem?

It is the employer's duty to accommodate employees' religious beliefs.

Are you bondable?

Defining Questions

Defining questions clarify hiring criteria, give the interviewer the opportunity to brag about the company, and set up your proof stories. Specific defining questions include the following:

1. What are your objectives for this position? What would you like to see accomplished by the person filling this position?

2. How does this position fit into the overall objectives or goals of your company?

3. What are you looking for this department/position to accomplish in the next year or so?

4. What principal skills are you looking for in the person selected for this position? What key technical, educational, or personal traits do you desire?

Controlling Questions

Controlling questions are a little trickier because they seek answers to those questions that are difficult to ask. When used effectively, controlling questions help you avoid ending up in a position where you might be unhappy or unsuccessful. Because of their potentially negative nature, use controlling questions selectively and sparingly, and only after there is a mutual conclusion that you are qualified for the job and have a sincere interest. Some of these questions may be used after an offer is made. Controlling question examples include:

1. Why is this position currently open? What happened to the incumbent? How long has it been open?
2. What is a typical career path for someone in this position?
3. What is the chain of command for this position? Who must approve my actions or decisions?
4. In the past, what has been your organization's response to economic downtrends?
5. What is the company's policy toward tuition assistance, military obligations, and release time for family matters?
6. What management style do personnel in this company employ?

Interviewing is a hectic but exciting time. Prepare for it, anticipate some setbacks, and try to relax and enjoy it.

USING YOUR PORTFOLIO

Chapter 7 discussed creating and using a career portfolio. As soon as you are comfortable in an interview, mention that you have brought some samples of your work for review. In a structured interview, you may be able to use the portfolio to help answer specific questions and provide proof of your skills and experience.

Let's say that you have asked the interviewer to describe his or her ideal candidate for the job, or perhaps you have asked the interviewer to discuss the top skills or traits desired for someone in the position. Once the recruiter has mentioned the desired skills or qualifications (which of course you have!) you can "make the sale" by proving that you have these characteristics, as demonstrated in your portfolio.

If you haven't had an opportunity during the actual interview to use the portfolio, don't worry. In such cases you can summarize why you are the best candidate for the position at the end of the interview and support this through the use of your portfolio. What a strong final impression that can make!

Next, we will discuss three important, but often overlooked, parts of an interview: etiquette, testing, and negotiating.

ETIQUETTE

Etiquette is worth mentioning here because during the interview process (particularly if the position sought has extensive client contact) a candidate may be taken out to lunch or dinner—and such dining events usually do not take place at McDonald's or Burger King. When a candidate is taken to lunch, she is being observed in a social setting. Your behaviour in this seemingly more casual environment is still part of the interview process. You are still proving yourself, just in a different setting. Follow your host's or hostess's lead on the price of the food ordered. Order something that is not too challenging to eat, and avoid messy "finger foods" like ribs or fried chicken. Also, do not smoke or drink alcohol during these meals.

Dining Etiquette

Although most people realize the importance of proper table manners, mastering them is a real art. Knowing the proper table manners is extremely important for job interviews and those social events you attend with a supervisor, client, or business associate. By being knowledgeable and practiced, you will avoid embarrassment and possibly offending someone.

Before the Meal

Men precede women to the table. Remain standing until the host or hostess is seated. During social occasions, it is still considered polite behaviour for a gentleman to seat his female guest or companion. When being seated, enter your chair from the left and rise from the right.

Napkins

Unfold your napkin immediately or after everyone is seated, and place it on your lap. Large napkins are typically left folded in half, with the crease toward you. Small napkins are completely unfolded. If you must leave the table during the meal, rest the napkin on your chair. At the end of the meal, place the napkin semi-folded to the left of your place setting, not on your plate.

Dining Tips

The following page offers a few tips to keep in mind.

Many other particular details are involved in proper dining etiquette. Before you begin your job search, do a little reading on proper dining etiquette. You'll be glad you did.

TESTING

There is a good chance that you will be expected to take tests as part of applying and interviewing for a job. Although many firms do not test at all, others rely on testing as screening and decision-making tools. Some tests may be oral questions during the interview, while others are written aptitude or technical tests. Still other testing is physical, such as drug tests.

Employers go to a substantial amount of trouble and expense to administer tests to candidates. Why? They use tests as tools to help them hire the best people possible—technically, intellectually, emotionally, ethically, and physically. There is really no way to prepare for these tests. All you can do is make sure you understand why a test is being administered, the conditions under which the test will be given, and the test directions. If you know about the testing ahead of time, get a good night's sleep so you are as relaxed as possible during the test.

Types of Tests

What types of tests can you expect to take? The following discussion covers the most frequently given test types.

Aptitude tests. These are tests of your general knowledge in such areas as word analogies, verbal comprehension, abstract reasoning, mathematics, and number and letter series. Included in this category are technical aptitude tests given to assess technical or subject area competencies.

Personality tests. On occasion, some psychological testing is done. These tests usually have the candidate react to a variety of questions or scenarios designed to categorize characteristics or behaviour types.

Technical tests. These may be oral or written and are used to assess the candidate's knowledge in his or her field.

Do

Sit up straight.

Keep your elbows in.

Wait until all are served before beginning to eat.

Use the silverware farthest from your plate first.

Pass to the right.

Cut only one or two small pieces of meat at a time.

Eat in small bites and slowly.

Place used silverware on the dish to which it belongs.

Replace your chair after the meal.

Don't

Place your elbows on the table while eating.

Wipe off your silverware before eating.

Reach in front of a person.

Help yourself from a dish first.

Bow down over the plate as you eat.

Blow on food to cool it.

Crumble your crackers into your soup.

Dunk.

Leave your spoon in your coffee, tea, or soup.

Stir beverages too vigorously.

Stack your dishes.

Drink or speak with food in your mouth.

Push your chair back after the meal and sit sideways or with legs crossed.

Drug tests. The most popular type of substance abuse testing is used to determine the amount of a substance or chemical in the body. (More details on this type of testing later.)

In addition, more companies are also requesting:

- Security clearances
- Criminal background check
- Driver's abstract

Tests can be administered in several ways. A general aptitude test is often a pencil-and-paper (or computerized) test. A technical test can also be pencil-and-paper or verbal, such as technical questions asked during an interview. Personality tests are usually pencil-and-paper tests; however, some candidates report having interviews with company psychologists to determine personality types and related behaviours. Because it is relatively inexpensive, the urinalysis is the most common type of drug test.

Test-Taking Tips

Keep in mind that no one can force you to take any type of test. You have the right to refuse a test; however, if you do, expect the interview process to end or be severely curtailed.

Before taking a test, ask how it will be scored or how the results will be measured. Will incorrect answers be subtracted from correct ones? Is there any penalty for guessing? Is it a timed test? Are unanswered questions marked wrong? Also, make sure you are given a quiet, distraction-free environment for taking the test.

For pencil-and-paper tests, keep a few basic rules of test taking in mind:

- Read the directions carefully before starting.
- If you are unsure of an answer, skip it and return to it later.
- For timed tests, make sure you are aware of how much time has passed.
- Read questions thoroughly; misread questions (or directions) can be disastrous.
- Your first answer is usually the correct one. Change test answers only when you are sure it is necessary.
- Dress appropriately. While you may not need to wear your interview suit, you don't want to call attention to yourself. This is still a component of the interview and you are being judged.

Some Thoughts on Drug Testing

Because employers want to employ individuals who will contribute to the company's productivity and profit, they do not want people with substance-abuse problems. Employees with serious substance-abuse problems may have more accidents, take more time off, and file more health insurance claims. Employers cannot afford these increased costs or the associated risks. Therefore, substance-abuse testing, particularly drug testing, is a part of the employment scene.

As mentioned previously, urine tests are the most common type of drug test. Before you give a urine sample, report any prescription drugs you are taking. It is also a good idea to mention any over-the-counter drugs that may be in your system. In addition, many people are not aware of the retention time many drugs have in the body.

Alcohol may have a retention time of up to 12 hours, while traces of marijuana can exist in the system for up to five days. Be aware that a reluctance to take a drug test will severely hurt or destroy your chances of employment. All testing, including drug testing, is serious business to employers.

Try to keep a positive attitude about any testing that is part of your job search. Whether you face an aptitude test, a personality test, a drug test, or all three, you have faced tests before and you survived just fine. Testing is just one more hurdle you must clear before you get the perfect job.

THANK-YOUS

One final activity is necessary to complete the interview process: you need to thank your interviewer. Although you have been thanking your interviewers all along throughout your interview process, a formal, final thank-you is still warranted. Which format is best for thank-yous—handwritten note card, typed letter, or an e-mail? This depends on the recruiter. You need to assess your situation and decide. Handwritten messages must be extremely legible and error free. Typed letters should be in a proper business writing format and error free. E-mails must be examples of good business writing and error free. Are you seeing a pattern here? Whichever method you choose for your thank-yous, make sure they are formal and professional in their look, tone, and style.

Now, you are finished with the interviews. The questions have been answered, the proof stories given, the tests taken, and the thank-yous sent. An offer (or two) is made! Now what?

Now is the time for contemplation. If you are fortunate enough to have two excellent prospects for employment, which one will you choose? What factors will be key in your decision? How will this decision affect you and your future? If you are thinking about a single offer, what is your gut feeling about accepting it? The next chapter discusses what you should do to make this all-important career decision.

MY Focus — ESPECIALLY FOR COLLEGE STUDENTS

The most obvious time to market yourself in the job-search process is during the interview. What an important sales meeting that is! Following are some characteristics of outstanding interviewees. Do these describe you?

- a smile and a pleasant disposition
- a businesslike and professional attitude
- eager and enthusiastic
- excellent appearance
- well spoken, articulate
- relaxed and poised demeanour, confident
- polite, ability to develop rapport
- sincere and honest
- good eye contact, attentiveness, good listening skills
- ease in answering questions

FINDING YOUR FOCUS

1. Why are behaviour-based questions the most difficult to answer well? What technique can you employ to structure and present effective answers to this type of interview question?

2. Go back to the section that discusses the questions you may ask in an interview. Select your top two standard, defining, and controlling questions. Why is each important to you?

3. How do you plan to respond to any illegal interview questions that are asked?

4. Work with a partner and ask each other behaviour-based interview questions. Assess each answer using the S.T.A.R. method. Was enough detail provided to demonstrate the proof?

After the Offer

After completing this chapter, you will be able to:

- Outline the basic realities of work.

- List four basic criteria for job evaluation.

- Apply criteria questions to your career decision making.

- Use both logic and emotion when deciding whether to accept a job offer.

- Explore personal salary expectations and develop realistic salary needs in order to negotiate more effectively.

- Describe the role benefits play in the negotiation process.

- Use appropriate negotiating techniques.

Making the Right Decision

Opportunity is missed by most people because it comes dressed in overalls and looks like work.

—THOMAS EDISON

After being in the job market for several months, Carol was tired. She had just finished a gruelling set of interviews, and was thankful she had no more scheduled that week. Even though she was tired, Carol was also excited because she had received a generous job offer from her top company. Things were looking good. But there was also a downside. Even though she was thrilled to get the offer, the job was slightly different from the type of work she did before. In addition, although the benefits were good and the company offered flextime, her commute was farther, costing her time and money.

Steve called his brother to discuss his new job offer. He was enthusiastic about the position and the company, and he saw plenty of room for career growth in the department. The job seemed interesting and challenging, but the company's location was the best part of all. The firm was literally three miles from his home, and he would be able to work from home on occasion. The only downside to the offer was the salary. It wasn't quite what Steve had in mind, even though he was assured that he would get a salary review after the first year.

As you can tell from each scenario, job offers often have both positive and negative aspects. This is fairly typical. Some job offers bring out different, sometimes conflicting, emotions in a candidate. Serious thought is necessary to make the right decision.

No matter whether you are looking for your first full-time career position or are making a career change, you may need to evaluate more than one job offer. What's the best way to do this? As you read this section, you will learn that the criteria for evaluating a job are fairly straightforward. What makes evaluating job offers difficult is that you are often comparing two or more offers that are never completely alike. As in the previous scenarios, there can be internal conflict about an offer. When comparing offers, use your head, your ability to reason, or logic as much as possible; however, ultimately, you may have to use your heart or gut—your emotions—to make that final decision.

139

WORK REALITIES

Here are a few common-sense, but sometimes overlooked, work realities.

1. We are all individuals who have our own values and preferences when it comes to work. What's right for one person may not be right for another.
2. The position you accept will to some extent affect your lifestyle, psychological well-being, and quality of life.
3. There is no such thing as a perfect job. Most jobs have less-than-perfect aspects.
4. Most positions today require 40 or more hours of work a week. In many cases, the 9-to-5 workday model is a thing of the past.
5. A large number of your waking hours per week are spent either at work or commuting to and from work.

With these realities in mind, let's examine some typical criteria for evaluating job offers. When you really think about it, there are four basic areas that should be examined when evaluating a job offer.

CRITERIA FOR EVALUATING A JOB OFFER

The following factors should be considered when you evaluate a job offer: the organization and its personnel; the scope of the job; salary and benefits; and the match between the job and your goals.

Let's take a closer look at how you can apply these criteria to your evaluation. To apply each criterion, several questions must be asked about the position.

The Organization and Its Personnel

- Is the company a reasonable distance from home?
- Are the physical facilities acceptable?
- Will I have the physical space and tools necessary for the job?
- Is the work environment formal or relaxed? What's my preference?
- Does the organization have a good reputation?
- Am I comfortable with the size of this organization?
- Am I in agreement with most company policies?
- Do people seem to remain with this company for a while?
- Will this position allow me to work as part of a team or individually? Which is more important to me?
- Do I see myself making friends with people in this company?

The Scope of the Job

- Does the position offer a variety of duties, or are there set duties that don't change? What is my preference?
- Will this position be challenging?
- What would a typical day, week, month be like?
- Will I use most of my skills and education?
- Does this position require travel? If so, what type and how much?
- What are the normal working hours? Is there flextime? Is there the possibility of telecommuting?
- Would I be happy getting up in the morning and coming to this job?

Salary and Benefits

- What is the salary for the job, and how does that compare with my needs and my analysis of the market?
- What size pay increase is typical?
- What intangibles should be considered along with salary?
- Does the firm offer competitive medical, dental, life, and other benefits?
- What are the company's profit sharing, pension or retirement plans, and stock offerings?
- What type of miscellaneous benefits come with this package (e.g., tuition reimbursement, daycare, bonuses, recreational programs, credit union)?

The Match between the Job and Your Goals

- Is there an opportunity for me to meet my long-term goals?
- What is the potential for job growth? Lateral movement?
- What are the schedule and criteria for my performance evaluation?
- Will I have the opportunity to learn new job skills?
- Does the company encourage continued education?
- Will this position provide an opportunity to meet other professionals in my field?
- Does this company support professional association membership?

Using the questions from these categories will help you make a well-informed decision about which job offer to accept. Compare each company using the four criteria and focus on the questions under each criterion that are the most important to you. This systematic approach can help with your decision making, but you may still have to consult with something else—your heart. After all is said and done, how do you feel about the opportunity? What is that little voice inside saying? What does your gut tell you? If you apply the typical evaluation criteria to a job (or two) and you still feel a bit of uncertainty, ask your heart, or tune into what your gut is telling you.

The Simplified Method

Another, simpler method of analyzing an offer or comparing two positions is to ask yourself the following basic questions:

- Can I do the work?
- Will I enjoy the work?
- Are these my kind of people?
- Is the job what I want?
- Does the job pay what I'm worth?
- What kind of person would I be working for?
- What sort of future can I expect with this firm?

A useful company evaluation exercise can be found on our **Companion Website**. In this exercise, a brief case study involving two different fictional companies' benefits, you compare the benefits and come up with the best choice for you.

No matter what method you use to evaluate a job offer, make your decision and stick with it. If you give the choice enough study and consideration, you will make the best decision. Don't be tempted to second-guess yourself. Decide and then look forward to a rewarding position that will move you toward your ultimate career goals.

NEGOTIATING

There are many aspects and nuances to proper negotiating during the job-search process.

The Issue of Money

For any job seeker, the issue of money is an important one. You want to sell your skills for the highest price or salary possible, and your potential employer wants to purchase your skills at a somewhat lower price. Remember, when the issue of money comes up, try to postpone it to a later time. Salary really isn't an appropriate topic for a first interview; you haven't decided if this is the position for you and the interviewer doesn't know yet if he is interested in employing you. Keep in mind, whoever talks about money first loses. If it's the employer, you have a more knowledgeable position to negotiate from. If you mention money first, you may mention a salary number or range that is either too high or too low. When you are in the interview, stress that you want to be a part of the firm so you can make a significant contribution. Let the interviewer bring up salary first.

If and when you are asked about your salary requirements, respond with a phrase like this: "Although salary is an important consideration, my primary interest is getting a career opportunity that benefits the company and gives me challenge and growth." If the interviewer is insistent about salary requirements, try asking "What is the salary range for the position?" Again, this deflects the mention of numbers back to him. If the range mentioned is acceptable to you, then tell the interviewer that it is in your range and continue the discussion.

Determining Your Salary

Determine your lowest acceptable salary before you get into a negotiating situation. If you do this, you can be more confident negotiating for a job you really want. Remember, a difference of a thousand dollars becomes negligible after it is divided by 26 pay periods, and taxes and benefit payments are taken out! In addition, with careful planning and successful work performance, you may be at a more desirable salary level within the first year or so.

Your salary expectations must be realistic. What is your desired salary or range and where did you get that figure? Are you basing it on the competitive rate that someone with your diploma, degree, and experience demands in the field? If so, then your number is probably right on. If you are basing your number on what "sounds good," it will not get you anywhere.

Several resources can help you determine this number: professional association surveys and member advice, information from individuals already in your field, and college or university career service offices or alumni associations. Don't forget to factor in cost of living for whichever region of the country (or the world) you intend to work in.

Compensation

So what exactly goes into determining a salary or salary range? What is considered compensation? When you think about your salary, consider your entire compensation package: your base salary, any variable or incentive pay you may receive as a bonus or performance incentive, and benefits. Typical company benefits include health, retirement, and paid time off. Others may include stock, a company car, tuition reimbursement, and child or elder care. There really is more to determining your salary or compensation than just the money you receive in your regular paycheque.

Considerations in Negotiating Salary

Consider several issues when negotiating salary and remain open to the offered salary until you have a chance to look at the entire benefits package. If, however, the salary offered is too low in your informed opinion, then you must speak up. You may register your disappointment in the amount offered (after continuing to point out your enthusiasm for the job offered), or you may indicate that the salary offered is not in line with what you believe is competitive in the field. Use these responses only when there is a considerable distance between what you were realistically expecting and what has been offered.

Considerations in Negotiating Benefits

It is also possible, in some cases, to negotiate benefits. In addition to the possible offer of a bonus as part of the compensation package, it may be appropriate to discuss additional funds for professional and personal development, extra vacation or insurance, and other options. Remember, these items should become an issue if you feel the salary offer is somewhat below your established market value. However, if you try this kind of negotiating when a fair salary offer has been made, it just may backfire! Some examples of benefits that may be negotiated are listed below.

Sample Benefits That May Be Negotiated

Athletic club membership

Bonuses

Company car, gas allowance

Consumer product discounts

Cost of living increases

Country club membership

Daycare

Dental plan

Disability pay

Drug plan

Educational fees

Extended health care—chiropractic, massage, physiotherapy, and other related benefits

Flexible work hours

Hospitalization

Housing

Investment programs

Legal assistance

Pension plan

Profit sharing

Relocation expenses

Retirement plan

Sales commission

Stock options

Travel

Vacation

Vacation discounts

Vision/Eye care

Wholesale buying

When to Negotiate

In addition to knowing what to negotiate, it is important to know when to negotiate. First, do not attempt to negotiate until a firm, defined offer is made. When considering negotiating, be aware of the condition of the economy and the job market. In a flush economy with more money and opportunities, negotiating may not be as risky and may be more successful. However, in a down economy, employers may not be willing or able to do much negotiating at all.

Recent graduates should not assume that their degree entitles them to a higher salary. Having your degree (or advanced degree) qualifies you for consideration for the position, and nothing more. If you have relatively little work experience in your field, your degree may keep you in the running, but it won't entitle you to a higher salary. At the same time, don't automatically assume that your degree is all you have to offer an employer. If you have some related work experience in addition to your degree, this carries more weight with an employer than the degree alone. Diplomas and degrees equal job-performance potential, while past job performance indicates previous work experience and achievements.

Negotiating Tips

- Know your market value before negotiating—do your research.
- Develop a personal budget to determine net salary requirements (don't forget taxes).
- Consider the total compensation package when evaluating an offer.
- Negotiate money first and benefits or perks later.
- Keep it friendly, personable, and non-demanding.
- Focus on your value to the firm and your role in helping the company meet its strategic goals.
- If you can't get more money, negotiate for future opportunities, responsibilities, scope of position—things that later translate into more money.
- Don't accept an offer on the spot; take some time to think about it.
- Consider accepting a lower salary if the secondary benefits can help advance your career or are a priority for you.
- Be sincere, honest, and honourable.

CONFIRMATION

Once you accept the position, confirm your acceptance in writing. If the firm has already sent you its offer in full detail in writing, you do not have to include all these terms in your letter. However, if you do not have anything in writing, you may wish to write an acceptance letter like the one in Chapter 6. In such a letter, you spell out essentials such as the position title and responsibilities, salary, start date, and location. This allows you to confirm that the details of the offer are exactly as you understand them.

After the offer is accepted, it is time to celebrate with family and friends! Finding a good job in any economy is an accomplishment, so enjoy it. And don't forget to let those who helped with your job search, such as contacts and references, in on the good news. Thank them again for their help.

MY *Focus*   ESPECIALLY FOR COLLEGE STUDENTS

When trying to make a decision between two offers, try this exercise. Take an 8 ½" × 11" piece of paper and fold it in half lengthwise. Write Company A's name on the top of one side and write Company B's name the same way on the reverse side.

To the left of the fold, write down all of the advantages you can think of for that position (and company). This is a brainstorming session, so don't hold back! Keep writing about positive things until you totally run out of ideas.

Once you have finished the positives, you are ready to consider the negatives. To the right of the fold, write down all of the disadvantages of the position. Again, keep the ideas rolling as nothing is insignificant at this point.

After listing as many positive and negative points as you can about each company, you can do one of two things to help with your analysis. First, simply observe which offer has the most positives in its column. Second, you can "cancel out" sets of positives and negatives. To do this, find a positive (good starting salary) and a negative (longer commute) of similar weight; for example:

Positive = great computer equipment/impressive office

Negative = no flextime or telecommuting

After doing this for each company, note what is left in the positive and negative columns. Considering that all other aspects have cancelled each other out, what's left? After this analysis, which position looks the best?

Keep in mind these two techniques are merely suggestions for a rather systematic approach to decision making. As stated earlier, decisions on employment are made with both the head and the heart!

FINDING YOUR FOCUS

1. List the four criteria for evaluating a job offer in the order of your personal priority. Explain your choice.

2. One part of a job offer evaluation is to consider whether it contributes to your long-term career goal. In a sentence or two, write your personal long-term career goal.

3. What are the top three benefits that are important to you as part of your personal compensation? Why?

4. What basic information should be confirmed in a job acceptance letter?

What to Know and Do

CHAPTER OBJECTIVES

After completing this chapter, you will be able to:

- Realize the importance of answering the question "Why do I work?"

- Demonstrate appropriate performance during your probationary period.

- Keep a log of personal accomplishments to use in your formal self-assessment.

- Realize the importance of the annual review to your career advancement.

- Determine what employees should not do while working.

- Apply the Tips for New Employees to your personal employment situation.

Maximizing Job Performance

The biggest mistake we could ever make in our lives is to think we work for anybody but ourselves.

—BRIAN TRACY

That first day on the new job finally arrived. You finished your orientation with the human resources department, met with your manager, and were introduced to some of your colleagues. You were shown your office or workstation and are now ready to get down to business. You are hopeful, excited, stimulated, determined, and maybe just a little nervous. All of these feelings are very typical when starting a new job. This chapter discusses what you must know and do as a new employee to start yourself off on the right foot and continue to travel down your personal path to success.

FITTING IN

Fitting into an organization and working well with people takes some effort. There is a breaking-in period for anyone in a new position. Even people who have been in previous professional positions have to earn their wings in a new work environment. Take time to learn the corporate culture. Become familiar with rules, values, behaviours, and expectations. Watch others. Notice who is successful and the techniques these people use. Adopt them and make them work for you. Always give a solid performance in everything you do, from a major project to a written memo. Hard work and the right attitude pay off. Learning how to fit in well in an organization is an initial step toward job satisfaction and career development.

What you should know as you begin your new job includes some ideas on what's important to you, how you will be assessed or evaluated, and the value of a mentor. You should also be aware of some good things you should do and some other things you should not do, and of tips for new (and not so new) employees.

WHAT'S IMPORTANT

First, let's explore what is important to you and how you define success. For most of us, it is important to be employed—to be working. However, different people take different things from their work. Ask yourself, "Why do I work?" "What benefits do I get from what I do on the job?" What is your personal definition of success in your work and your life? Is it having a high salary and good benefits that provide for you and your family? Is it the professional pride you get from being respected for your work? Would you call success your ability to advance into higher positions of responsibility and compensation? How you see your reason for working and how you define your personal success have a lot to do with how you will approach your work and prepare for your future.

ASSESSMENT

One important thing to know about your job is how you will be assessed or evaluated. As a new employee, you may have a probationary period when you first start working.

Probationary Period

How long is this probationary period? In many companies, this is the first few months or so, when you may be learning the ropes of your job and establishing your typical work behaviours and practices. During this probationary time, you may be given some special assistance or help. Typically, you and your work are looked at more closely than after you become a seasoned employee.

Don't let this idea scare you. It is a very typical procedure. A probationary period is not a problem if an employee is working hard and doing his best to be a productive part of the department or company. However, if a new employee is not completing tasks on time, is spending work time on personal matters, is tardy or has excessive absenteeism, the firm may re-evaluate his position in the company. So, during your first several months of employment in particular, show them the best you've got. Be a model citizen of the organization.

Performance Review

Probationary period or not, you will have a formal evaluation of your work from time to time. In most organizations, this happens once a year and may be called a performance review. If you have had these reviews before, you already have an idea of how these written tools assess your work, and of the role they play in determining future pay raises and promotions.

Because this assessment usually happens only once a year, keep a record of the projects you did, the kudos you received, and the specific ways you contributed to the department and the company overall. Keep a log of these efforts and save samples of any notable written work you created or to which you contributed. This type of personal file is extremely valuable later on, particularly if you are asked to do any type of self-assessment or self-evaluation. These self-assessments are routinely asked for by managers to help them prepare their employees' annual performance reviews. So, as you begin performing in your new work environment, remember that you will eventually be evaluated. Be as prepared as possible to help your manager give you the glowing performance evaluation that you deserve!

THE VALUE OF A MENTOR

Another idea to consider as you begin your new employment is to seek out a mentor in the organization. A mentor is someone who can assist you when you have questions, guide you along in your new work environment, and serve as a type of role model. A mentor can be someone you admire and wish to emulate. A mentor can be someone who has achieved success in the organization and can teach you some of the ways to be successful in that particular environment or field. Observe the people around you. Who seems to be successful and admirable? Whom would you like to seek out for advice? Selecting and using a mentor in your career can bring you many great benefits.

Either through your immediate manager or perhaps your mentor, find out about your career path in the organization. What is the next position you could aspire to? What is a typical career path for someone in your position, and how long does it usually take to get to the next level? What type of training or education is necessary to get promoted? Who can help you prepare your career path? This is all very worthwhile information to gather.

GOOD THINGS TO DO IN A NEW JOB

Following are some good things to do in a new job.

- Understand your probationary period.
- Come prepared with a journal to write down important points in your training. Not only will it make a good impression but you will need to refer back to this information.
- Record important information on a daily basis in a journal. This documentation can be invaluable at a later date if asked to clarify or recap information.
- Keep a log of your accomplishments and activities in preparation for your annual review.
- Find a mentor.
- Find out about your career path and how it can be achieved.

THINGS TO AVOID DOING IN A NEW JOB

It may seem strange to discuss some things you should *not* do. However, sometimes what seems to be common sense to us may not be quite that common. The qualities discussed below are sure-fire ways *not* to impress a new employer and can lead to serious problems.

Dishonesty and lying. If an employee lacks integrity, most all other qualities are meaningless.

Irresponsibility, goofing off, attending to personal business on company time. One who wastes the company's resources and is unreliable may not be trustworthy.

Arrogance, egotism, and excessive aggressiveness. There is nothing redeeming about someone who spends more time bragging or boasting than working, or one who feels she deserves special treatment or privileges.

Absenteeism and lateness. If employees are chronically late or absent, most employers feel they don't deserve to be paid for time they did not work and work they did not do.

Other undesirable traits include not following instructions, ignoring company policies, laziness, lack of enthusiasm, making ill-informed decisions, and taking credit for work done by others.

COMPUTERS: THE NEW PITFALL

In the last couple of years more people have lost their jobs for a specific reason—improper use of computers—than ever before. You need to understand that many companies are now developing zero-tolerance policies for misuse of computers. Among the behaviours that companies are not tolerating are these:

- Visiting inappropriate Internet sites
- Visiting any site not directly related to company business
- Downloading programs or software not authorized
- Installation of software not authorized
- Receiving or forwarding e-mails unrelated to company business
- Playing games on company computers

Recently in one medium-sized company, for instance, 10 people within a seven-month period were fired for violation of the company computer policy.

Many companies can track the websites you've visited, the length of time you've spent there, the programs you've downloaded or installed, and what you've received and forwarded in your e-mail. This is the new reality.

GENERATIONAL DIFFERENCES

Understanding the dynamics of the workplace may make it easier to ensure your success. There has been a lot written about generational differences in the

EXHIBIT 11.1   **Generational differences**

	Traditionalist	Baby Boomer	Gen X	Millennial
Approximately When Born	1925–1945	1945–1964	1965–1980	1981–2000
Major Influences	Depression Pearl Harbor World War II Korean War Radio	Vietnam War Sexual revolution Civil rights Feminism Space travel Rock & roll Television	Personal computers Video games MTV Latch-key kids Divorce increase	School shootings Internet Cell phones Terrorism Multiculturalism Protection from parents
Key Traits	Hard workers Dedicated Sacrifice Conformity	Optimism Team workers Loyal Career driven	Seek work/life balance Fun Independent Techno savvy Multitasker	Realists Respect for diversity Very confident Civic minded Achievement oriented
What Matters at Work	Department & organizational goals Policies & procedures Big picture Respect	Challenges Recognition Personal growth Lifelong learning Relationships Loyalty	Work/life balance Training and development Access to information Constructive feedback Hands-off supervision Work should be fun	Mentoring Training Personal goals Respect for authority must be earned
Preferred Communication	Memos, face to face	In person, meetings	E-mail	Instant Messenger

workplace. Exhibit 11.1 is meant as a guideline only. Experts in the field often differ in their research but overall this information should assist you in understanding and working in an intergenerational workplace.

Conflict in the Workplace

Dealing with conflict in the workplace can be one of the most challenging issues and cause more stress than almost anything else.

While the above chart may be useful as a first step in understanding the potential reasons for some interpersonal problems, there are many other issues that can cause conflict in the workplace. Simply, different personality types work differently. Workplaces need diversity in order to operate effectively. Almost everyone brings strengths and weaknesses to the workplace and learning how to recognize each person for what they bring to the team can make a huge difference to the efficiency of that team.

Sometimes you will come across someone who is just difficult to get along with. If this is constant then it is probably something you need to work on. I recall a story of someone who was having a difficult time working with an individual and then discovered through conversation they had a common love of Golden Retriever dogs. Once this connection was made they were able to move forward in their working relationship.

Sometimes you will find that someone is rude to you or snaps at you for no apparent reason. Tell yourself at this point that the person's behaviour is probably not related to what happened at that moment but rather that they may be stressed out by something else. Go back and discuss the incident with that person at a later time.

Respecting everyone you work with will often help you avoid conflict of any kind. One last tip is to thank people for assisting you—even if it is part of their job. A simple "thank you" goes a long way toward avoiding conflict in the workplace.

JOB SAFETY

A section on job success would not be complete without some information on job safety. It is important to realize that you have rights and you should never be exposed to an unsafe work environment. In Canada, occupational health and safety legislation protects you against hazards on the job. In addition, each province has its own legislation. You and your employer are jointly responsible for workplace health and safety.

Know Your Rights

Starting a new job is very exciting, but it can also be a bit overwhelming. After all, you're meeting new people and worrying about making a good impression in front of your boss and co-workers. With all that pressure, don't forget to ask about your basic rights when it comes to workplace safety. You owe it to yourself to know your rights!

Know Your Responsibilities

As an employee you have many rights, but you also have many responsibilities. By being responsible in the workplace, you can help avoid injury.

Follow All Safety Rules

The old saying "rules are meant to be broken" definitely does not apply to workplace safety. You may be tempted at times to take shortcuts, but at the end of the day, you were trained a certain way for a reason: to keep all your body parts intact! If you have not received health and safety training, let your employer know right away.

Report Hazards

No one likes to be a snitch, but when it comes to workplace safety it's your responsibility to report potentially hazardous situations. Just imagine how you'd feel if someone got seriously injured because you didn't want to make a report.

Protect Yourself

Gloves, masks, safety boots, and other protective gear may not look cool, but if the job requires it, you've got to wear it. You should also never remove a guard or device designed to protect you. That's the law. No job is worth risking your life.

How to Refuse Work

If you have reason to believe that your workplace is unsafe, you have the right to refuse to work. You should always try to get your employer to correct the unsafe work situation first.

Physical Hazards

Physical hazards are very common in most workplaces. They are easy to spot, but surprisingly, often overlooked. They can cause injury, illness, and even death.

Types of physical hazards to look out for:

- Electrical hazards
- Unguarded machinery
- Constant loud noise
- High exposure to sunlight/ultraviolet rays, heat or cold
- Working from heights or any raised work area
- Working with mobile equipment

Chemical Hazards

Some chemicals are safer than others, but for workers who are sensitive to chemicals, even common solutions can cause illness, such as skin irritation or breathing problems.

Types of chemical hazards to look out for:

- Cleaning products, paints, acids, and especially chemicals in an unlabelled container
- Gases like acetylene, propane, carbon monoxide, and helium
- Flammable materials like gasoline and solvents and explosive chemicals

Musculoskeletal Disorder Hazards

Musculoskeletal disorder hazards are conditions that pose the risk of injury to your musculoskeletal system. These types of hazards are tough to spot because you don't always immediately notice the strain you're putting on your body. Short-term exposure may result in sore muscles, but long-term exposure can result in more serious injuries.

Types of musculoskeletal disorder hazards to look out for:

- Poor lighting
- Improperly adjusted workstations and chairs
- Frequent lifting
- Awkward posture
- Awkward movements, especially if they are repetitive and forceful

Biological Hazards

Biological hazards are typically found when working with animals, people, or infectious plant materials.

Types of biological hazards to look out for:

- Blood or other body fluids
- Fungi
- Bacteria and viruses
- Mould
- Insect bites

THE 3 R'S TO SAFETY

Recognize the Hazard

You know that feeling you sometimes get in the pit of your stomach when something doesn't seem quite right? Learn to pay attention to it! While some hazards are easy to spot, there are many hidden hazards that fly under the radar—like faulty equipment or machinery. You should report all potential hazards as soon as you sense that something is wrong.

Report the Hazard

Reporting a workplace hazard is the only way the problem can get fixed. After all, your boss isn't a mind reader—how can something get fixed if he or she doesn't even know about it? By reporting a hazard you'll not only be protecting yourself, you'll also be protecting your co-workers.

Remove or Resolve the Hazard

Once you report a hazard, it's up to your boss to ensure that the problem gets resolved. This can include everything from adding a protective metal guard to the installation of proper ventilation—it varies from situation to situation. If the problem isn't properly addressed, you have the right to refuse to work.

The 3 R's to Safety reprinted with permission from WSIB Ontario.

Your Rights

- You have the right to refuse unsafe work.
- You have the right to safety training.
- You have the right to know actual and potential dangers in the workplace.

Your Responsibilities

- To work in compliance with regulations
- To use personal safety equipment and clothing as directed by the employer
- To report workplace hazards and dangers

The Canadian Centre for Occupational Health and Safety has a website (www.ccohs.ca) that provides a wealth of information on this topic as well as links to many other sites.

HARASSMENT IN THE WORKPLACE

Employers in Canada are required by law to develop and enforce harassment policies. Every employee is protected by this policy and also responsible for following the policy to ensure a respectful workplace. This sounds ideal, doesn't it? As with any other policy or law, unfortunately, not every person or employer will comply. Again, the best way you can protect yourself is to understand your rights and responsibilities.

As defined by the Canadian Human Rights Commission, harassment is any behaviour that demeans, humiliates, or embarrasses a person, and that a reasonable person should have known would be unwelcome. It includes actions (e.g., touching, pushing), comments (e.g., jokes, name-calling), or displays (e.g., posters, cartoons). The Canadian Human Rights Act prohibits harassment related to race, national or ethnic origin, colour, religion, age, sex, marital status, family status, disability, pardoned conviction, or sexual orientation.

Some of the above definition may be surprising to you. What may have been acceptable behaviour within your group of friends may not be acceptable in the workplace. You must remember that this is all about having a respectful workplace. For more information on harassment, go to www.chrc-ccdp.ca/publications/anti_harassment_toc-en.asp#12.

Steps to Take If You Are Harassed

You may also wonder what actions you should take should you find that you are being harassed in the workplace.

- First, you should let the person know that you find their behaviour offensive and you wish it to stop.
- Your next step, if it does not stop or you are not comfortable speaking directly to the offender, should be to report the action to a supervisor, the human resource department, a union representative, or the person designated in your company policy. Remember, you are protected by the law and this is your right.

For further information please go directly to the Canadian Human Rights Commission website, www.chrc-ccdp.ca/default-en.asp.

CLOSING ADVICE

The box below offers tips for new (and not so new) employees. To some of you, this advice may seem like common sense. However, most of us can benefit from it.

In addition to these tips, there are some additional considerations: Set your own personal work goals, be willing to put in long days, make sure your dress is appropriate for your office and the dress code, limit personal calls and other communications, observe proper business meeting etiquette, learn how to handle stress and work overloads, foster positive business relationships, and seek a

Tips for New Employees

- Watch how things are done in the company. Observe the business culture and how people interact personally.

- Be sensitive to a diverse work culture. Because you will be working with people from different ethnic and cultural backgrounds, you must understand the different ways others think, communicate, and act.

- Be respectful of others' time. Use it wisely and don't assume it is owed to you. Time is precious to everyone, especially in today's fast-paced and demanding business world.

- Be careful with the way you use communication technology. It can be your best friend or your enemy. Electronic business communications should be professional, clear, concise, and correct.

- Understand that you will make mistakes, but realize that's how you learn. A wise person once said that mistakes are just lessons you haven't learned yet.

balance in your life. This advice is useful for all of us to keep in mind, whether we are new employees or experienced professionals!

Obviously, there is a lot more to know and do as a new employee, but, hopefully, this chapter touches on some of the most important considerations. Your work ethic, your personal and professional standards, and your treatment of others all combine to make you who you are on and off the job. You are working for a variety of reasons. Your work is a major part of your life. Work hard and enjoy the benefits. Work is an essential ingredient to success. In the words of Mark Twain, "The dictionary is the only place where success comes before work."

MY Focus ESPECIALLY FOR COLLEGE STUDENTS

Following are ways you can implement some of the suggestions found in this chapter.

Make a list of traits you feel a good employee must have. You may use traits from the chapter and include your own original ones. After each trait, indicate the level (on a scale of 1 to 10, with 10 being the best or highest) that best reflects your level of that trait. If you rank a trait low for yourself, write a suggestion as to how you could make yourself stronger in that trait.

Join a professional organization that relates to your field. (Many employers will pay for professional memberships for employees.) Get to know individuals in that organization who may serve as mentors or guides for your own career. Ask your potential mentor if you could shadow him or her sometime to see how he or she performs on the job.

The night before you start your new job, create a folder to bring to your office. This folder can have a descriptive title such as "Brag Folder" or "My Best Stuff" or even "What I've Done All Year." Place the folder in a convenient but discreet spot and remind yourself to place material in it when appropriate.

FINDING YOUR FOCUS

1. What is your personal definition of success and how will it guide you in your new job?

2. What is your impression of a probationary period for employees? Is it warranted? Unfair? Why?

3. If you have experienced performance reviews before, what is your opinion of them? How are they useful? How can they be damaging?

4. Review the Tips for New Employees in this chapter. Which do you consider to be the top two to keep in mind?

5. What are your three safety rights?

6. Write down one person you know from each of the generations described above. Determine whether their traits match those in the chart. What tip would you provide for working with that person?

12

Career Success Skills

CHAPTER OBJECTIVES

After completing this chapter, you will be able to:

- List the basic career skills necessary for top job performance and career success.

- Apply the top 10 traits employers seek to your personal profile of traits.

- Recognize the difference between employee skills and personal values and characteristics.

Being the Best You Can Be

Let us realize that the privilege to work is a gift, that power to work is a blessing, that love of work is success.

—DAVID O. McKAY

You've finally made it through the process. You successfully assessed and marketed yourself, and assembled and used marketing tools to get the job you wanted. You interviewed well and convinced the employer that you were the best person for the job. You have a good idea of what to do on the job to maximize job performance. There is just one more thing to keep in mind: career success skills. These skills don't pertain just to new employees. They are relevant for new, experienced, and even senior-level employees. They are called career success skills because they are extremely important in the work setting. They can be considered life success skills as well.

So, what are some of these career success skills? There has been much written about the skills and traits that employers want today. Although no two lists of desirable skills or traits are the same, many share similar qualities. A couple of these lists appear later in this chapter, but for now let's examine some of the basic skills that are desirable in any work environment.

BASIC SKILLS

If you saw a list of the most basic career success skills, the list would look something like this: reading, writing, speaking, listening, teamwork, and problem solving or creativity. You may have expected to see the first four skills, but might have been a little surprised by the last two. Let's take a look at each individually.

Reading

This seems pretty basic, doesn't it? Actually, this refers not only to the reading skills one uses on the job, but also to the ability to read and learn in general. With all of the information at our fingertips in today's technological world, how does one stay ahead? Employees must be able to read, skim, summarize, synthesize, and manipulate what they read. They must have a strong vocabulary, not only in their own field, but in business, industry, technology, and even in science. Reading is essential to learning.

Writing

Writing has always been essential to conveying ideas or informing, persuading, and communicating on a personal basis. In today's culture of electronic written communications such as e-mail, writing has continued to be an important skill. From creating basic business correspondence (memos, letters, proposals, reports) to creating and sending electronic information, employees must have good writing skills. Of course, clear writing reflects clear thinking, so these two skills go hand in hand.

The three key features critical to successful writing on the job are clarity, conciseness, and correctness. Successful writers present their ideas clearly. They know how to communicate ideas carefully and accurately. Good writers are also concise. No one has time to read through unnecessary words or ideas. Although conciseness in writing has always been important, in today's fast-paced world, being able to communicate ideas in a streamlined yet complete manner is essential. Correctness is another factor of successful communication skills. Our image is reflected in how we communicate. If our writing is full of mechanical errors and awkward wording, our readers will not think much of our message or us.

Speaking

This skill goes beyond public speaking. Although public speaking can be key to your future career success in some instances, your general interpersonal communication skills are on display all the time. In addition to being able to compose and deliver a good speech to an audience, you must be skilled and confident when addressing smaller groups of people during a business meeting, business luncheon, or professional conference. Just as you may be judged by the clothes you wear, you are always being evaluated by your speech.

Listening

Not much is said or taught about the skill of listening. But consider this: you probably spend a large part of your day on the job listening to people—in meetings, personal conversations, on the telephone, and talking to clients. Listening is a skill—and an important one. Successful listeners give their complete attention to the speaker. At the same time, they mentally summarize what the speaker is saying, analyze the information, and formulate a clear response to the message. The ability to listen is a critical skill that all employees must have. Miscommunication in the workplace can be very costly on many levels.

Teamwork

Some time ago, the average worker was able to do her job alone. No one else was needed. The individual worker knew all that was necessary to get the job done. Fast forward to today. The world, and particularly the business world, is full of complexities and rapidly evolving innovation. One person alone doesn't have all of the knowledge and skills to get the job done. Increasingly, grouping workers into teams has been necessary to share knowledge and information as the team moves toward a common goal.

What does it take to work well in teams? It takes an understanding of different communication styles, particularly those of people from diverse cultures. It takes a willingness to share responsibility and accountability. It requires that you practise give-and-take, and sometimes conflict resolution, to solve problems and continue to move forward. Teamwork allows us to share one another's talents. Teamwork skills are highly sought after by today's employers.

Problem Solving and Creativity

In today's complex society and global marketplace, companies need employees who are equipped to solve problems efficiently and effectively. They need people who can take data/facts/information, draw conclusions, and make appropriate recommendations. They need people with fresh approaches to situations, people who can handle change and the challenges of a global marketplace. Thinking "outside of the box" is important in a society where creativity is required to solve challenging problems.

SPECIFIC SKILL SETS

The comments so far have covered some of the basic career success skills that are important in any type of workplace and any field of endeavour. But what are some of the specific skill sets that employers say they want in employees? What skill sets will guarantee your personal success in your career?

Skills Needed to Get Ahead

The first list of skills needed to get ahead in the current work culture was mentioned in a presentation given by Dr. Phillip D. Gardner, Research Director at the Collegiate Employment Research Institute at Michigan State Universities. Following are some of the conclusions from that presentation:

- In today's workplace, everyone has to be professional.
- Learning is now a job requirement, and employees must have mental agility.
- The linear thinking of yesterday will not work with the abstract systems of today.
- Employees must be aware of and learn from the gurus in their fields.
- Employees need organizational savvy in order to get things done.
- Employees need to go well beyond their typical job descriptions to be successful.
- The more you know and can do successfully on the job, the more freedom, flexibility, and autonomy you are given.

Finally, Dr. Gardner indicates that in the workplace of today and the future, with our culture stuck in fast-forward, the important thing is not what you know, but rather how quickly you can innovate.

Another list of employee traits was found in an article published by a U.S. university system. The article summarizes 10 capabilities looked for by corporations in their new employees.*

Top 10 Traits Employers Seek

1. **Excellent verbal and written skills.** Employers emphasize the ability to communicate clearly to teammates, peers, superiors, and subordinates.
2. **Ability to turn theory into practice.** Higher-level thinking is always desirable; however, companies need personnel who can put into practice what they know, people who can get results.
3. **Working well in groups.** Companies want team players. Employers often want employees who can work well in teams of four to six people. Such teamwork also requires that team members be able to function well with those of different ethnic and social backgrounds.
4. **Flexibility.** Rapid advances in technology and customer needs combine to make constant demands on companies and their employees. Employees

*Adapted from pamphlet *Survival of the Fittest*, published originally by DeVry University.

must be able to adapt to and use new structures, programs, and procedures. They should be flexible and willing to change as needed.

5. **Problem solving.** Critical-thinking skills and good communication skills are essential for today's employees. They must be able to recognize, define, and solve work-related problems efficiently and effectively.

6. **Creativity.** Employers value those who can go beyond currently accepted models to find original solutions. Realizing that each challenge requires a unique answer, individuals must have the confidence needed to take risks and try new and different ideas.

7. **Living a balanced life.** Today's world is full of stresses. How you deal with these stresses helps to determine who and what you are. Those who lead lives balanced with outside recreational and social activities are better adjusted and more productive workers.

8. **Time management.** Managing time and meeting schedules and deadlines are important. Competing responsibilities and multiple work tasks can often be challenging. Effective employees are those who handle their responsibilities dependably and in an efficient manner.

9. **Fearlessness.** Although employers do not want reckless behaviour in their employees, they do find that breakthrough successes require professionals who are not afraid of failure. Also, employees who do fail must learn from those failures, adapt, and try again.

10. **Commitment.** Being committed and dedicated to corporate or group goals is crucial. Loyalty and goal orientation are key traits. Employees possessing these traits are seen as cornerstones of the corporation. These are the individuals who are responsible for the company's long-range success.

Skills and Values Prized by Employers

A final list of skills and values prized by employers is presented in an article entitled "What Do Employers *Really* Want? Top Skills and Values Employers Seek from Job-Seekers" by Randall S. Hansen and Katharine Hansen.* Their discussion of skills and values prized by employers is summarized here.

Skills Mentioned Most Frequently

According to the Hansens, studies have identified several important employee skills, sometimes called soft skills due to their nontechnical nature. The following list includes those skills mentioned most frequently by employers.

1. *Communication skills (listening, verbal, written).* This was the one skill mentioned most often.

2. *Analytical/research skills.* Individuals must be able to assess situations, seek different perspectives, and identify key issues.

3. *Computer/technical literary.* A basic understanding of software and hardware, such as word processing, spreadsheets, and e-mail, is required.

4. *Flexibility/adaptability/managing multiple priorities.* This is the ability to handle multiple assignments, set priorities, and adapt to change.

---

*Copyright by Quintessential Careers and found at QuintCareers.com, an online career-development webpage. Used with permission.

5. *Interpersonal abilities.* The ability to relate to co-workers, inspire others, and manage conflict.

6. *Leadership/management skills.* This includes taking charge and managing workers.

7. *Multicultural sensitivity/awareness.* Some feel that there is no bigger issue in the workplace than diversity. Employees must show an awareness of and sensitivity to other people and cultures.

8. *Planning/organizing.* The ability to design, plan, organize, and implement projects; includes goal setting.

9. *Problem solving/reasoning/creativity.* Solving problems with powers of creativity, reasoning, and past experiences in combination with available information and resources.

10. *Teamwork.* The ability to work with others in a professional manner while working toward a common goal.

Personal Values Employers Seek

In their article, the Hansens also present a list of personal values employers want in their employees. Although the specific skills already mentioned are critical to career success, what the employee is or values is as important as what he can do. Values, personality traits, and personal characteristics are also critically important to career success and satisfaction. Following are some values mentioned in the Hansens' article.

1. *Honesty/integrity/morality.* Employers probably respect personal integrity more than any other value.

2. *Adaptability/flexibility.* Being open to new ideas, working in teams or alone, multitasking.

3. *Dedication/hard work/work ethic/tenacity.* Employers want and value employees who love what they do and will stick with the job until it's done.

4. *Dependability/reliability/responsibility.* Punctual employees who have a keen sense of responsibility.

5. *Loyalty.* Devotion to the company under a variety of conditions.

6. *Positive attitude/motivation/energy/passion.* These are people with drive and passion, who show enthusiasm with their words and actions.

7. *Professionalism.* Acting in a responsible and fair way, signs of maturity and self-confidence, lack of pettiness.

8. *Self-confidence.* Obvious belief in what you can do and in your mix of skills, education, and abilities.

9. *Self-motivation/ability to work with little or no supervision.* Although teamwork is a coveted ability, so is the ability to work independently with minimal direction.

10. *Willingness to learn.* No matter the employee's age or experience, an open attitude to learning new skills or techniques is vital.

Being the best you can be on the job requires much of you. You must cultivate the skills and traits most prized by employers and personify the values and attitudes that lead to success on the job. With the right combination of these skills, traits, personal values, and attitudes, you will be successful in achieving long-term career growth and personal satisfaction.

MY *Focus* — ESPECIALLY FOR COLLEGE STUDENTS

Several lists of desirable skills and traits have been discussed in this chapter. Review the lists, and make your own list of the ones that were mentioned the most.

Next, circle the ones you feel you currently possess to a high degree. Next, take a look at the other skills and think about how you may work at developing these.

A variation on this activity is to involve a peer or co-worker who knows you and your work well. Ask this person to write down a list of your most prominent work traits, skills, and attitudes. Compare this list to the lists in this chapter and see which ones others believe you possess. Note the ones you still need to work on.

FINDING YOUR FOCUS

1. Using the following skills discussed at the beginning of the chapter, rank them in order of importance according to your personal experience. Be able to justify your ranking.

   _____ reading

   _____ writing

   _____ speaking

   _____ listening

   _____ teamwork

   _____ problem solving/creativity

2. According to the Hansens' article, a fact in today's workplace is that "everyone has to be professional." What does it mean to you to be professional? Ask others and see if their definitions agree with yours.

3. Define agility. Why is that a necessary skill for today's employees?

4. Commitment to the company is a skill that is desired by employers today. Does this desire seem realistic considering the tendency of many employees to change jobs and companies rather frequently? Do you feel the value of commitment to a company is important? Why or why not?

INDEX